PRAISE

"In *Billion Dollar Purpose*, Leila Lahbabi redefines what it means to scale. This is not a manual for faster growth but a manifesto for meaningful impact. With clarity, depth, and strategic precision, she bridges timeless principles with actionable frameworks, empowering leaders to build businesses that last. If you believe that profitability and purpose are not mutually exclusive but mutually reinforcing, this book will become your blueprint. It's not just about transformation; it *is* the transformation."

–Caroline Libeau | Entrepreneur

"We have all seen it, founders numb their souls in their journey to achieve impact and greatness. It triggers their companies to lose their spark as these grow. Leila shows how to scale without numbing founders' souls. Mission, energy, passion all fuel Founders' souls. Maintaining the associated spark ensures both founders' personal and company growth. This is about how you grow your soul, not just your company."

–Abdelaziz Yatribi | Founder & CEO of Yamna | Global green hydrogen and derivatives development and investment company committed to drive the energy transition revolution.

"In this book, Leila Lahbabi explains with great simplicity the secret sauce of a true impactful leader. More than just driving profits and creating employment, a true leader knows how to connect deeply with themselves and the people in their organizations. If you have the courage to be one, you shouldn't miss this book."

–Paula Sancho | Venture Capital | Partner Finaves

BILLION-DOLLAR PURPOSE

How Conscious Leaders Scale Impact and Win Without Burnout by Attracting, Retaining, and Developing High-Performing Teams

LEÏLA LAHBABI

Billion-Dollar Purpose
How Conscious Leaders Scale Impact and Win Without Burnout by Attracting, Retaining, and Developing High-Performing Teams

ISBN: 979-8-89079-285-3 (hardcover)
ISBN: 979-8-89079-286-0 (paperback)
ISBN: 979-8-89079-287-7 (ebook)

Leadership Awake Press

Legal and Earnings Disclaimer

While all attempts have been made to verify the information provided in these materials and their ancillary materials, neither the author nor the publisher assumes any responsibility for errors, inaccuracies, or omissions and is not responsible for any financial loss incurred by the reader in any manner. Any references to people, companies, or organizations are purely coincidental and unintentional. If legal, financial, or professional advice is needed, the services of a qualified professional should be sought. The information contained in this book is strictly for educational purposes. Therefore, if you wish to apply any ideas contained in these materials, you do so at your own risk and take full responsibility for your actions.

Neither the author nor the publisher purports this book to be a "get-rich scheme," nor do they guarantee, either expressly or implicitly, that readers will achieve specific results using the strategies, concepts, techniques, and ideas presented. Earnings and outcomes are dependent entirely on the efforts, skills, and circumstances of the individual applying the material. Any examples, stories, or case studies included are for illustrative purposes only and should not be interpreted as typical results. No representations in any part of these materials are promises of actual performance. The strategies and statements offered are based on opinion and experience and should not be misinterpreted as guarantees of success.

This book and its associated materials are not intended as a source of professional financial, legal, business, personal, or medical advice. Readers should be aware of the various laws governing business transactions and practices in their respective jurisdictions. The author and publisher disclaim any warranties (express or implied), including but not limited to warranties of merchantability or fitness for any particular purpose. Under no circumstances shall the author, publisher, or their representatives be liable to any party (including third parties) for any direct, indirect, punitive, special, incidental, or consequential damages arising from the use of this material. This content is provided "as is" without any warranties.

HELLO AND WELCOME!

I'm so glad you've chosen to explore this book, and I'm excited to share this journey with you. Whether you're here to bridge profit and purpose, inspire growth, or build high-performing teams, these pages will offer valuable insights and strategic frameworks that you can apply right away.

This book is about creating sustainable, long-term impact through purpose-driven leadership. It's based on real-life business experiences, successes, failures, and lessons learned from high-growth companies, mission-driven founders, and forward-thinking investors.

The idea of *Billion-Dollar Purpose* is about scaling businesses that create massive financial and societal impact. Whether through a single high-growth company or a network of mission-driven businesses, the future belongs to those who integrate purpose with sustainable profitability.

When I began the journey of writing this book, I set out to explore how businesses can truly thrive by focusing on their most valuable asset: people. We live in a world where technology races ahead, yet the human element remains at the heart of any successful business.

In these pages, you'll discover the leadership strategies, counterintuitive scaling methods, and talent-building frameworks that will help you drive sustainable, high-performance growth without burnout or compromise.

This book is for people like you: leaders who believe that scaling a business is about creating environments where people grow, innovation flourishes, and collective purpose drives long-term success. It's a call to action for visionary leaders who want to inspire, scale their impact, and build a legacy that thrives through the years.

To support you in applying these ideas, I've created the Billion-Dollar Purpose Cheatsheets, a practical companion to this book. They provide clarity and focus, ensuring you can quickly reference key takeaways and implement them in your business. Download them here:

leilalahbabi.com/billiondollarpurposecheatsheets

These cheat sheets are designed to provide clarity and focus, ensuring that you can quickly reference the most important takeaways without sifting through pages. Most importantly, these cheat sheets will help you bridge the gap between learning and action, allowing you to scale your profit and purpose with clarity, confidence, and impact.

Enjoy the journey, embrace the learning, and remember: Scaling with purpose is not just possible; it's the future of business.

Let's begin.

To those who believe that people are the greatest investment.

To the dreamers who challenge the status quo, the leaders who scale with vision, and the changemakers who build legacies beyond profit.

And to my family and friends, your unwavering support fuels this journey.

This book is for you.

FOREWORD
BY ELISABETH MORENO

There are two types of leaders: those who follow pre-established paths and those who redefine them. If you are holding this book in your hands, it means you belong to the second category. You understand that entrepreneurship is not just about building a company but it's about creating a legacy, an impact, a vision that transcends your own journey.

Today's business world is saturated with conversations about growth, performance, and efficiency. But too often, this relentless pursuit of success comes at the cost of something essential: purpose. In the frenzy of short-term gains, many entrepreneurs forget why they started in the first place. They sacrifice their vision on the altar of immediate profitability, failing to realize that the companies that truly change the world are the ones that, first and foremost, change lives.

Simon Sinek speaks about the difference between finite and infinite games. Too many businesses operate as if success were a sprint, a race to maximize quarterly earnings, to outpace competitors at any cost, to chase immediate wins. But true, enduring leadership is an infinite game. It's about building something that lasts, something that continues to grow, adapt, and make a difference long after the initial rush of success fades. It's about playing for legacy, not just for the next financial report.

Leila Lahbabi offers us more than just a strategic guide. Billion Dollar Purpose is an invitation to rethink leadership, to restore the true meaning of success. This book proves that impact and profitability are not enemies but powerful forces that, when aligned, amplify each other. It reminds us that real growth is not just measured in numbers but in the value we create, the communities we build, and the lives we transform.

A truly sustainable business is not built on spreadsheets, it is built on vision. A vision carried forward by engaged teams, by leadership that does not simply manage but inspires, elevates, and unites. This book will teach you how to attract top talent, how to build a company culture that outlasts trends, and how to create an organization that not only thrives but leaves a lasting impact.

If you are looking for a guide to scale at any cost, this is not the book for you. But if you want to build something that outlives you, if you believe that success can and must have meaning, then this book will be an invaluable compass.

The greatest entrepreneurial revolutions are not born from a frantic race for profit. They emerge from a relentless desire to change the game, to reinvent, to challenge the status quo. This book is a declaration of war on outdated models. It is a promise that, yes, a new kind of leadership is possible.

The future belongs to those who dare to create it.

So, are you ready to be part of the change?

–Elisabeth Moreno

FOREWORD
BY JERRY COLONNA

THE PURPOSE-BUILT LEGACY

There comes a moment in the life of every leader—a reckoning of sorts. A moment when they look around at the business they've built, at the people who rely on them, at the weight of the responsibilities they carry, and they feel something stir inside them. It's not doubt, exactly, nor is it fear. It's something quieter, more persistent, and it can gnaw at them. Oftentimes its quiet little voice whispering *Is this what I set out to build?*

This question rarely arrives at the beginning of a journey. In the early days, founders and leaders are fueled by the momentum of creation. They push. They drive others forward and they often end up carrying the weight of the company's success—or failure--on their shoulders. They build, they scale, they stretch toward growth. They do what is required of them—until one day, they wake up to find that what once felt expansive now feels confining. That the business they labored to bring into the world has become something else entirely—something consuming, something exhausting, something that no longer quite resembles the vision they once held so clearly.

This is the crucible of leadership.

Warren Bennis wrote that true leadership is forged in the crucible, in the moments of adversity and transformation when leaders are forced to confront not just the external challenges of their work, but the deeper internal reckonings that shape them. The question, then, is not *How do I scale?* but *How do I scale without losing myself? How do I build something great without burning it all down in the process?*

It's at this juncture—this moment of reckoning—that *Billion Dollar Purpose* arrives like a clear voice in a fogged-over room.

Leila Lahbabi has spent years watching founders, CEOs, and teams wrestle with these questions. She's seen what happens when leaders try to muscle their way through scaling, when they treat growth as an act of sheer will rather than an act of intention. She's also seen the alternative: leaders who build companies that last because they understand that real success isn't measured in short-term wins, but in sustained, purpose-driven impact.

This book is not just another guide to scaling a business. It's a manifesto for a different way of leading, a blueprint for those who refuse to choose between impact and profitability, between sustainability and success. It challenges the relentless, extraction-driven models of leadership that have left so many founders and executives exhausted, and it offers something far more valuable in return: a way to scale without losing your soul in the process.

THE FALLACY OF MORE

In my years of coaching leaders, I have seen time and again how easily we fall into the trap of believing that *more* is always the answer. More revenue, more headcount, more expansion, more effort. But what I have also seen—what I have learned firsthand—is that growth, without clarity of purpose, becomes its own form of entrapment.

Leila understands this. She knows that scaling isn't just about getting bigger, but about getting *better*. That adding people to a team without tending to the culture only leads to dysfunction. That pursuing revenue without a clear mission creates a business that may be profitable but not enduring. That a founder who scales their company without scaling themselves will inevitably find that they've built a machine they no longer know how to operate—or worse, a machine that no longer serves a good greater than their own wealth, their own pursuit of more.

It's here that *Billion Dollar Purpose* shines.

Leila doesn't just offer strategies; she offers a shift in perspective. She challenges leaders to move beyond transactional leadership and into something more transformational. She reminds us that businesses are not just systems and structures, but living, breathing organisms—ecosystems of people, ideas, and values. She calls leaders to embrace what she defines as collective *intelligence*—the understanding that sustainable success is not built on the genius of one individual, but on the synergy of a team that is empowered, aligned, and fully engaged.

THE LEADER'S RECKONING

There's an uncomfortable truth that most leaders eventually face: the skills that got them here will not get them where they need to go.

The founder who was once the scrappy, all-hands-on-deck force behind the company's birth cannot remain at the center of every decision as the organization grows. The CEO who built their reputation on relentless execution must eventually learn to step back, to delegate, to trust. The leader who once prided themselves on their ability to push through exhaustion must recognize that burnout is not a badge of honor, but a warning sign.

To scale successfully, a leader must also scale themselves.

This is one of the most powerful insights in *Billion Dollar Purpose*: the recognition that scaling is not just an external process, but an internal one. That leaders must grow in proportion to the businesses they build. That they must learn to let go of control in order to foster real, sustainable leadership within their teams. That their job is not just to build a business, but to build a culture that can thrive beyond them.

BUILDING TO LAST

There's an old proverb that says: *A society grows great when old men plant trees in whose shade they will never sit.* The same is true for leadership. The best leaders are not the ones who burn themselves out in service of short-term gains, but the ones who build something that will outlast them, a purpose-built legacy.

Leila understands this. That is why this book is not about quick hacks or unsustainable scaling tactics. It is about laying foundations. About creating organizations where people don't just work but thrive. About fostering leadership that is not extractive, but regenerative. About ensuring that the legacy a leader leaves behind is not just financial, but cultural.

Reading *Billion Dollar Purpose*, I was struck by the depth of its wisdom. This is not a book written from the sidelines, but from the trenches. Every insight, every strategy, every framework has been forged in the real world—through the successes and failures of high-growth companies, through the lessons learned by leaders who have walked this path before.

If you are a founder standing at the crossroads, wondering how to grow without losing yourself in the process, this book is for you. If you are a CEO who has built something successful but longs to make it meaningful, this book is for you. If you are a leader who wants to leave behind more than just revenue numbers, who wants to build a company that stands for something, who wants to scale not just for the sake of growth but for the sake of impact—this book is for you.

The world does not need more businesses that grow at all costs. The cost to our communities and our planet of such a mindset is too great. What we need are businesses that grow with purpose. What we need are more leaders who understand that scaling is not just about expansion, but about endurance. What we need are founders who are willing to ask themselves not just *How do I succeed?* but *What do I want to leave behind?*

This book is a guide for those leaders. It is a blueprint for those who are ready to scale in a way that lasts.

And if you are holding this book in your hands, it means you are ready to begin.

–Jerry Colonna, CEO Reboot.io and author of
Reunion: Leadership and the Longing to Belong and
Reboot: Leadership and the Art of Growing Up

TABLE OF CONTENTS

INTRODUCTION

PART 1
SHIFTING THE WORLD
BY SCALING THE RIGHT WAY

PART 2
HOW TO SCALE YOUR
BILLION-DOLLAR PURPOSE

INTRODUCTION

WHY THIS BOOK IS RIGHT ON TIME

Less than 1 percent of companies successfully scale. Investors report that 65 percent of scale-up failures happen due to leadership and organizational issues, including weak executive teams, lack of delegation, and misaligned growth strategies.

Having a great product, market fit, or even funding is not enough to scale. It's important to build the right leadership, culture, and team to sustain that growth.

Most companies struggle to scale, not because they lack strategy or capital but because they don't have the right people in place to execute at scale. This book is here to change that.

Scaling your business in alignment with your mission, values, and purpose is essential for long-term success. When we scale purpose-driven companies and build a billion-dollar purpose economy, we create massive value without relying on businesses that prioritize profit at the expense of people or the planet or out of fear of political uncertainties.

WHY TALENT IS THE KEY TO SCALING

Many founders think scaling is about systems, processes, and efficiency. While these are important, they are not the real bottleneck.

Think of scaling like building a house. I could teach you about the best materials, architectural design, and structural engineering, just as many business books teach systems and strategy. However, when it comes time to build, you'll be overwhelmed:

- Where do you start?
- How long will it take?
- How do you ensure it's executed properly?
- How many skills do you need to learn before you can even begin?

Trying to master every skill yourself is a recipe for burnout, frustration, and stagnation. Instead of building alone, what if you could attract and activate the best builders, people who understand your vision and are eager to help you bring it to life?

This is what scaling through talent means. Your people are your biggest asset if you have the right ones in the right roles working in synergy.

But let's be honest, recruitment is one of the riskiest and most costly investments a business makes:

- Hiring a new employee can cost three to four times the position's salary (SHRM, 2022).

- A bad hire impacts productivity, increases supervision time, and adds replacement costs.

- New employees take months to reach full productivity, often straining existing staff.

- Poor onboarding further raises turnover, amplifying recruitment challenges.

Also, managing people can be one of the most difficult challenges you face if you're not prepared:

- Poor management increases stress and inefficiency: 84 percent of employees say untrained managers create unnecessary work and stress (SHRM).

- Workplace conflict is common: 85 percent of employees experience workplace conflicts, affecting morale and productivity. (Pollack Peacebuilding).

- Disengagement and turnover are costly: Only 33 percent of employees feel engaged at work, while poor management contributes to high turnover and even health risks (Gallup, Niagara Institute).

The difference between thriving and struggling often comes down to whether your team is a source of momentum or a burden weighing you down.

Your success relies on your people. Make sure they are:

- In the right places, with the right skills

- A return on investment, not a drain on resources

- Well-compensated and valued, so they stay and grow with you

If you want to grow, you don't have to do it alone.

If you want to grow, you can't do it alone.

Scaling succeeds when a committed team works together toward a greater mission.

Purpose-Driven Companies Outperform Profit-Driven Ones

In addition to being good for the world, purpose-driven companies can also outperform traditional businesses financially. Data shows that mission-driven businesses outperform traditional ones financially by ten times (Firms of Endearment).

They don't just attract customers; they build movements. They don't just hire employees; they create high-performing cultures.

Companies like Patagonia, Salesforce, AirBnB, and Toyota prove that doing good and doing well are not mutually exclusive.

It's Time to Scale the Right Way

If you're reading this, you already have a big vision. You're seeing results. You've gained traction. But you know that continuing to operate the same way isn't sustainable.

Scaling isn't a sprint; it's a marathon. And if you're running at full speed without the right preparation, how far can you really go?

This book will guide you step by step to scale your business and impact without compromising your mission, your values, or your well-being.

The world needs more businesses like yours—companies that serve a higher purpose, create financial success, and contribute to a better future. You don't have to burn yourself or your team out to make that happen.

It's time to innovate the way we operate, scale with purpose, and build a future worth living in.

PURPOSE-DRIVEN
OUTPERFORMS PROFIT DRIVEN

"One hand doesn't clap on its own."

This is one of my favorite Moroccan proverbs because it captures the essence of cooperation, the key to growing and scaling your business.

The journey of attracting and training high-performing talent cultivates something deeper within your company than simply ticking boxes or achieving KPIs. Attracting and retaining high-performing talent is a way to make your company thrive with purpose without burning out.

This book is about the power of talent—and what it takes to scale successfully and sustainably.

I use the word "talent" rather than "employees" throughout this book because I want you to think inclusively about the different ways talent can help you scale your business regardless of the type of contracts you have with them.

This is so important because:

- Only 1 percent of companies manage to scale.

- Eighty percent of startups fail, not because of the market or product but because of the lack of leadership, poor decision-making, and fragile group cohesion.

- Purpose-driven companies have ten times the financial performance of most companies on the S&P 500, and this is my ambition for yours.

- Twenty to twenty-five percent of a company's valuation during due diligence is based on its people.

- Unaddressed conflicts within companies are costly (30 percent loss in productivity and 50 percent of talent leave because of conflicts). In the US alone, companies lose an average of 2.8 hours per week per talent dealing with conflicts, which results in a loss of $359 billion in lost productivity annually (CPP Inc.).

THE CLAP FRAMEWORK: SCALING THE RIGHT WAY

When I consult with organizations or speak from the stage, I often use the acronym CLAP to help my clients or audience understand the power of what I'm sharing.

- **C – Collective Intelligence**: Companies with strong collective performance experience a 20 percent increase in profitability (Deloitte).

- **L – Leadership:** Companies with strong leadership development see a 30 percent improvement in performance (McKinsey).

- **A – Autonomy:** Autonomous teams experience a 40 percent productivity increase compared to centrally controlled ones (MIT Sloan Review).

- **P – People:** Talent retention and engagement enable an increase of 21 percent in productivity (Gallup).

Bonus: S – Sustainability: When you compound the benefits of CLAP over time, you create repeatable success. Companies that build sustainable talent and leadership foundations scale exponentially over time.

The numbers are exciting!

By compounding those effects, your company can multiply its performance 2.6 times year after year.

That can mean as much as 100 times performance improvement over the next five years!

This is the power of exponential sustainable growth.

(When I say performance, I mean the combination of profitability, financial gains, productivity, and the impact of your products, services, and message on the world.)

SCALING WITH PURPOSE STARTS NOW

So, as you move forward, I encourage you to keep one key thought in mind: Enjoy the journey. Whether it's the small victories, the challenging moments, or the milestones that define your company's growth, each step brings you closer to building something remarkable, lasting, and truly impactful.

Here's to the future you're creating, one intentional step at a time.

WHY I'M WRITING THIS BOOK

In my former life, I was helping Fortune 100 CEOs develop their business strategies. But no matter how brilliant the strategy, I kept seeing the same problems:

- Great ideas weren't getting implemented.
- People resisted change because they didn't feel valued.
- A relentless focus on profit led to disengagement.

Then, there was the burnout, so much burnout.

It wasn't just the people around me; I felt it, too.

But here's the thing: It wasn't from the hard work. It was because:

1. Values were out of alignment.
2. Leadership has been told and believed that this way of operating was the only way to ensure the business or organization would grow

Good news! This is not true.

Scaling a business doesn't have to cost you your well-being, your values, or your team's engagement.

There are proven ways to grow profitably *and* sustainably.

FROM BURNOUT TO PURPOSE-DRIVEN SCALING

That realization pushed me into transformation. I had to overcome stress and burnout and redefine what success meant.

And I discovered something powerful:

- When I take care of myself, I become a better leader, consultant, and speaker.

- You can scale a company without sacrificing your personal life.

- Fulfillment and fun are not just nice-to-haves; they are essential for long-term success.

I started teaching these principles to my clients. However, over time, I realized something:

Helping one person at a time wasn't enough because:

- Too many leaders with enormous potential struggle at work.

- Most people want to work in environments that align with their values and mission.

- Founders burn out in the scaling phase because they fail to delegate or surround themselves with the right team.

So I started asking myself, "How can I make a bigger impact? How can I help purpose-driven companies scale sustainable businesses without burning out their leaders and their people?"

That's when I came up with the concept of the Billion-Dollar Purpose Approach.

THE MISSING LINK IN SCALING: YOUR PEOPLE

I've spent years refining the strategies that make companies successful.

I know what works, how to grow, how to make profits, and how to enter new markets.

However, over time, I realized that no amount of outer work will succeed without inner work.

Companies without aligned leadership, without a strong culture, and without a sense of responsibility for their people don't make it in the long run.

I've seen it over and over.

Here's the reality: It's critical to attract and retain high-performing talent to scale your growth, profitability, and impact without burning out.

It makes sense, right?

However, it's more complex than it appears because:

1. For younger generations, the average tenure is just 24 months. This means that building talent retention and engagement isn't just a nice-to-have; it's critical for long-term success.

2. Yes, you want to attract and retain high performers, but you don't want to burn them out.

3. Turnover is expensive. Losing talent can cost 50 percent to 200 percent of their annual salary. That's not a risk companies can afford to keep taking.

4. Technology can duplicate processes, but it's *human creativity* that drives innovation. That's why getting the right people in the right places has an exponentially positive impact.

5. A values-driven, sustainable business model is central to all of this.

I'm writing this book because too many founders and CEOs are:

- Scaling without a clear strategy for leadership and talent

- Burning themselves (and their teams) out in the process

- Losing sight of why they started in the first place

I wrote this book to change that.

I want to help purpose-driven companies scale profitably, sustainably, and with impact.

What You'll Discover

This book will show you how to:

- Reposition your role within your company so you can lead with clarity and focus.

- Build, train, and grow a high-performing team that can carry your mission forward.

- Develop adaptive leadership and measurable results.
- Scale sustainably, profitably, and with purpose—without burnout.

The future of business belongs to those who scale with purpose.

Let's build it together.

HOW CAN WE BUILD BILLION-DOLLAR PURPOSE TOGETHER?

Imagine the tiny cells inside a caterpillar, which are known as *imaginal cells*. These special cells carry the blueprint for something extraordinary: a butterfly. At first, they operate independently, each one acting as a single-cell organism.

However, the caterpillar's immune system sees them as threats and tries to destroy them.

Still, the imaginal cells persist. They multiply, connect, and begin to communicate with each other, sharing information and energy.

Slowly, they start to act not as isolated cells but as a unified system. Then, something remarkable happens: They reach a tipping point. The cells synchronize, and together, they transform the caterpillar into a butterfly.

THE IMAGINAL CELLS OF BUSINESS TRANSFORMATION

In many ways, purpose-driven leaders are like these imaginal cells within our society:

- They hold the vision for transformation, even when the systems around them resist change.

- They see potential where others see limits.

- They connect with others who share that vision, multiplying their impact.

Today, we are experiencing a global awakening in business.

Despite the noise of fear, greed, overconsumption, and short-termism, something powerful is happening: Purpose-driven leaders, companies, and investors are coming together and forming a movement that is reshaping the future of business.

This is the moment of metamorphosis where profit and purpose work together to create long-term prosperity.

WHO THIS BOOK IS FOR

I've written this book for the imaginal cells of today's business world, those leading the transformation:

- Purpose-driven executives, founders, and business owners who want to scale profit with purpose and build businesses that last

- Impact investors who want to support purpose-driven companies in scaling their sustainable growth while continuing to make a return

- Purpose-driven talent who want to contribute to the success of mission-aligned companies while growing in meaningful careers

Together, let's scale billions of dollars of purpose-driven economy.

Don't compromise on your values.

Innovate.

Have fun.

The time is now.

HOW TO USE THIS BOOK

If you believe that billions of dollars in economic growth should come from creating real value for customers, talent, and the planet, then you're in the right place.

This book offers a practical approach you can start using right away. It is built on years of experience, real-world success stories, and insights from leading companies and executives. It will challenge outdated business strategies and introduce a scalable, purpose-driven approach to growth.

Inside, you'll find:

- Timeless principles that apply across industries, regions, and company sizes
- Stories, questions, and action steps to help you reflect, grow, and implement
- Real-world case studies and cautionary tales to show what works—and what doesn't

This book is divided into two parts.

PART ONE: THE PARADIGM SHIFT

This section redefines how we approach talent, leadership, and sustainable growth and how this new definition helps scale profit with purpose. It challenges traditional myths, introduces new metaphors, and shares inspirations from companies that are winning with this approach.

By the end of this section, you'll understand the concrete benefits of implementing each step of the approach and why this creates more profitable and sustainable growth for purpose-driven businesses than conventional strategies.

PART TWO: THE IMPLEMENTATION GUIDE

This section provides a step-by-step framework for applying these principles in your business. It includes:

- Actionable strategies for attracting, training, and retaining high-performing talent

- Real-world case studies that make each step practical and concrete

- A structured process for measuring performance, ensuring that your investments in talent translate into profitable, purpose-driven, and sustainable results

TAKING ACTION

To make it even easier to put these ideas into action, I've created a free, downloadable resource with:

- Actionable frameworks

- Key takeaways
- Practical tools to help you implement these insights immediately

Download yours here:
leilalahbabi.com/billiondollarpurposecheatsheets

Start Scaling With Purpose

Whether you're an executive, founder, or investor, this book will help you scale your impact by building high-performing teams.

My hope is that you'll blend these strategies with your vision to create the influence and impact you're aiming for.

Let's begin.

PART 1

SHIFTING THE WORLD BY SCALING THE RIGHT WAY

"We make a living by what we get, but we make a life by what we give."

—*Winston Churchill*

I've always been inspired by the butterfly effect, the idea that a small action can create massive consequences.

In business, there is no such thing as a "small" company. Every decision, every investment in people, and every act of service creates a ripple effect that extends far beyond the walls of your organization.

When done right, business is a vehicle for delivering value to humanity. It enables individuals to come together, combining their unique strengths to create products and services that enhance lives and reshape industries.

But scaling the right way is key.

When purpose-driven businesses grow, power shifts into the hands of leaders who prioritize people, innovation, and sustainability rather than profit at any cost. This creates a virtuous cycle where high-performing talent, customers, and investors align around a shared mission.

That's why this book is for companies at all stages as long as you're committed to scaling sustainably, attracting aligned talent, and delivering real value to the world—because your business is not just about what you sell but the impact you create.

MOST FOUNDERS, CEOS, AND LEADERS ARE DOING IT WRONG

The way most businesses approach scaling doesn't work.

Only 1 percent of companies successfully scale. The problem isn't the market. It's not even the product. It's the people.

Too many businesses treat talent as an afterthought, assuming that growth is just about processes and operations.

However, here's the reality:

- Companies that invest in their people thrive. High-performing, engaged teams drive better products, services, and profits with joy.

- Joyful workers create stronger families, communities, and economies.

- The workplace shapes how people feel about their lives. People spend most of their waking hours at work. When they're engaged and valued, society benefits as a whole.

When businesses create human-centered cultures where talent grows mentally, emotionally, and professionally, the world gets better, not just inside companies but far beyond them.

Purpose-driven businesses are proving that doing good and doing well are not mutually exclusive.

So, what if your company was a place where:

- Talent was excited to join, stay, grow, and create massive value?

- Your team was aligned in purpose, values, and impact?

- You weren't scaling alone but were part of a network of purpose-driven businesses that amplify each other's success?

This is the bigger picture, and it starts with you.

SNAPSHOT: THE BILLION-DOLLAR PURPOSE APPROACH

N o great success happens in isolation.

When you surround yourself with the right, aligned people, your ability to scale increases exponentially.

As I shared earlier, "One hand doesn't clap on its own."

But here's the catch.

It's not just about your recruitment process or what you do. It's about who you are as a company and the value you deliver and multiply.

That's why The Billion-Dollar Purpose Approach takes a holistic approach, addressing both the internal and external dimensions of your business.

This book will guide you through five crucial steps to scaling sustainably without burnout, inefficiency, or losing your mission.

FIVE STEPS TO SCALE SUSTAINABLY

If you've reached a certain level of success, it means you've found market fit and achieved great things. When you identify and address the scalable areas in your business with this method, you will be able to scale further, stepping away from day-to-day operations and focusing on your sustainable growth.

In a nutshell, the Billion-Dollar Purpose Approach can be summarized in five steps:

- Step 1 – Scale Your Mission: Align and evolve your company's purpose to attract talent, customers, and investors.

- Step 2 – Scale Your Talent Attraction and Retention: Build a thriving, mission-driven workforce that stays.

- Step 3 – Scale Yourself as a CEO: Grow your leadership so your company doesn't outgrow you.

- Step 4 – Scale Your Team Performance: Develop a high-impact, self-led team that drives results.

- Step 5 – Scale Your Adaptability: Build a company that thrives in changing markets, with or without you.

Throughout this book, you'll find real-world case studies and frameworks to help you implement these principles.

I invite you to look at each example with a beginner's mind because you may not like every aspect of each company. (Neither do I.)

However, what's important here is to extract what will most help your business and people thrive.

We'll continue to unpack this approach, layer by layer, throughout the book.

In the meantime, if you haven't downloaded the Billion-Dollar Purpose Cheatsheets to turn these insights into actionable results, you can get them here:
leilalahbabi.com/billiondollarpurposecheatsheets

THE FIVE BIGGEST
SCALING MYTHS

In my years of helping businesses grow and scale, I keep seeing businesses getting stuck and leaders not stepping into their full potential.

Like so much of life and business, it's the myths, misperceptions, and misunderstandings that are causing this.

While these aren't the only myths, they are the biggest ones. But the key is this: When you're operating from fear, on autopilot, or stuck in outdated beliefs, you're holding your business and your people back from what they can truly become.

Instead, when you know the truth, so much more is possible!

Myth #1: To scale, you just need to hire the most skilled people and offer the highest salaries.

Reality: People who come for money leave for money.

What really matters is attracting and retaining talent who believe in your mission. Values-aligned, purpose-driven talent stay and give their best because they're aligned with your company's values and vision, not just their paycheck. This is not an excuse to make an economy of not paying your talent well or not looking for the best; incompetency and bad operations cost more. This is an invitation to build a movement that attracts the right fit.

Myth #2: Recruitment is the key to a strong workforce, and there is a talent war.

Reality: Retention and clarity are your true competitive advantage.

The true strength of your organization lies in its ability to retain the right talent over the long term, not in being the most aggressive recruiter. There's plenty of talent out there, but if you don't know exactly what kind of person fits your vision and mission and you are not able to retain them, you'll keep missing the mark and repeating an endless cycle of recruiting and firing.

Myth #3: Scaling a company just means growing operations.

Reality: Scaling requires scaling yourself first.

As your company grows, so do the challenges, pressure, and responsibilities on the founders. Founders who don't develop their emotional resilience and leadership skills in alignment with who they are often find themselves overwhelmed, and this stress permeates the entire organization.

Myth #4: The more talent you have, the more you can deliver.

Reality: Scaling your team means empowering their growth.

Scaling isn't about getting bigger; it's about increasing your impact. A huge, inefficient organization will drastically increase your operating costs and lower your profitability. A lean, talented, focused, and self-led team that lives by your mission will outperform a bloated organization every time and increase your return on investment.

Myth #5: Adaptability is about reacting quickly to change.

Reality: Adaptability thrives on proactive growth.

True adaptability is rooted in collective intelligence: the ability of your team to collaborate, innovate, and proactively find solutions before problems arise.

We'll unpack those myths throughout this book while providing concrete steps to scaling your business profit with purpose and talent alignment without burning out.

STOP KISSING BURNOUT

"I can't step away from my business for long, or it'll die. All this talk about relaxing doesn't make sense. Who will run my business while I'm relaxing? People who say that probably don't understand how hard it is to run a business or how reactive you need to be to keep it from going under."

These are the words from a dear friend, a founder of a green-hydrogen business who described himself as "kissing burnout."

As a founder, you cannot push yourself to burn out all the time. It is also difficult to take a break from the business to relax if it cannot run by itself. Recruiting people is not enough because when you have a large team, you also have more responsibilities and operating costs, so there is more pressure on the results. This is especially the case when you recruit people to tell them what to do because your team will then always rely on you to tell them what to do.

This is where the power of a self-led team comes in, and this is part of why the five steps of the approach in this book will help you.

I want better for you. You don't have to constantly hustle or sacrifice your well-being, nor do you need to disconnect from your emotions.

There is a leaner, more sustainable way to scale your business that allows you to maintain its longevity, feel fulfilled in serving the world, and have the energy to keep going for years to come.

With this approach, you'll even have the freedom to step away from your business if and when you choose while it continues to thrive without you. (This will be the focus of step five, but you need to master the first four steps to make it happen.)

LIKE PEELING AN ONION

Truly creating impact at scale is kind of like peeling an onion.

There are many layers.

I've discovered from working with an array of people and businesses that understanding the approach works best going step by step.

So, before the deep dive, let's peel back just a few more layers.

It is important to take the steps of the approach in the following order. Each step is a prerequisite to the success of the next one. For example, to enable your team to make decisions at their level, it is important to ensure an alignment on the mission first.

STEP 1: SCALE YOUR MISSION

Scaling your mission means refining and evolving it as your company grows. This involves reassessing your purpose, integrating stakeholder voices, and clarifying key areas of focus.

As an example, Patagonia scaled its mission from outdoor gear to environmental activism, embedding sustainability into its business model. This shift attracted values-aligned customers, strengthened employee commitment, and fueled long-term success.

The result? Patagonia's mission alignment delivered tangible business advantages:

- Over $1 billion annual revenue, proving that mission-driven brands attract loyal, high-value customers

- Four percent employee turnover, demonstrating that a strong mission fosters retention and a high-performing culture

- Over $100 million donated to environmental causes, reinforcing Patagonia's brand credibility and impact, which in turn strengthens customer and stakeholder trust

Patagonia's success proves that a well-defined mission is a powerful growth strategy. Here's how you can apply this approach to your company:

- **Strengthen Alignment:** Your mission evolves with your business. If it stays stagnant, misalignment creeps in, creating inefficiencies, leadership gaps, and disengaged employees. The key is to reassess your mission regularly so it remains a north star for growth. Why this matters:

  o Prevents misalignment between leadership, teams, and stakeholders

  o Transforms your mission into a decision-making compass

  o Attracts high-performing talent who align with your values o Reduces inefficiencies, such as hiring misaligned employees or facing internal conflicts

When your mission evolves alongside your business, you increase performance, create a thriving workplace, and scale with purpose.

- **Integrate the Voice of Stakeholders:** Your mission doesn't exist in a vacuum. Engaging with stakeholders transforms it from an internal statement to an external movement, attracting mission-aligned clients, partners, and investors who actively support your growth.

By deeply understanding stakeholder needs and aligning them with your purpose, you build:

o Client loyalty: Customers become brand advocates.

o Stronger partnerships: Reliable suppliers who prioritize your business.

o Investor trust: Shareholders who believe in your long-term vision.

This trust and alignment create a solid foundation for scaling, reducing marketing and operational costs, and strengthening your long-term impact.

- **Clarify Your Areas of Focus:** Scaling isn't just about growing for the sake of growth; it's about growing in the right direction.

Why focus is essential:

o Helps avoid overextension and resource drain.

o Increases resilience by ensuring alignment with your core purpose.

o Supports innovation while staying mission-driven.

Having a clear focus on your leverage points allows you to scale sustainably without losing sight of what matters most.

Scaling your mission means evolving your purpose to stay relevant and impactful. When your mission aligns with your growth strategy, it becomes a catalyst for scaling sustainably, attracting top talent, and driving long-term success.

In Part 2 – Step 1, we'll go deeper into how mission clarity can be your most powerful asset for growth.

STEP 2: SCALE YOUR TALENT ATTRACTION AND RETENTION

Scaling your talent attraction and retention means prioritizing retention as a competitive advantage, building a values-driven brand and culture, and hiring and onboarding the right fit.

Salesforce exemplifies how a strong cultural framework can attract and retain high-performing talent. Its "Ohana" culture emphasizes trust, customer success, innovation, and equality, fostering an environment where employees are empowered to excel and become brand advocates.

The result? Salesforce's talent strategy delivered measurable business advantages:

• Retention improved as employees aligned with the company's values, contributing to sustained innovation.

- Revenue growth accelerated, with annual revenue increasing from $1.65 billion in 2010 to $34.86 billion in 2024.

- Market capitalization expanded significantly, growing from $17.34 billion in 2010 to over $310 billion by February 2025.

Salesforce's success demonstrates that scaling talent is about building an environment where the right people stay, thrive, and drive innovation. The good news is you can apply the same principles to your organization.

Here's how you can do it:

- **Retention Is Your Biggest Competitive Advantage:** Constantly replacing employees drains resources, slows momentum, and fractures team culture. The real advantage lies in keeping the right people. Retention matters more than recruitment because it:

  o Drives long-term growth: Mission-aligned employees become experts, drive innovation, and create lasting impact.

  o Stabilizes operations: A retained workforce reduces disruptions and keeps teams focused on strategic goals.

  o Saves significant costs: Turnover can cost 50 percent to 200 percent of an employee's annual salary (SHRM).

  o Boosts morale and efficiency: Frequent hiring cycles erode culture, slow down projects, and reduce overall productivity.

○ Retention isn't just a cost-saving measure; it's a performance multiplier.

- **Build Your Brand and Culture Based on Authentic Values:** A thriving workplace starts with genuinely lived values. Employees who feel a deep connection to your mission engage more, collaborate better, and stay longer. Values strengthen retention by:

  ○ Increasing loyalty: Employees who believe in the mission stay committed and motivated.

  ○ Boosting collaboration: Shared values create a supportive and productive work environment.

  ○ Reducing hiring struggles: Values-aligned employees advocate for your brand and attract like-minded talent effortlessly.

  ○ Transforming employees into ambassadors: Retained employees spread your company culture organically.

- **Attract and Onboard the Right Fits:** Attracting the right talent is only half the battle; onboarding is what turns new hires into long-term contributors. Onboarding matters for retention because it:

  ○ Drives faster productivity: A strong onboarding experience accelerates integration and performance.

  ○ Improves retention rates: Employees with structured onboarding are 69 percent more likely to stay for three years.

o Strengthens employer brand: Well-integrated employees become company advocates, making future hiring easier.

o Prevents cultural misalignment: Effective onboarding ensures new hires fit seamlessly into the company's values and mission.

We'll go deeper later in the book.

STEP 3: SCALE YOURSELF AS A CEO

Scaling your company requires scaling yourself first. As your business grows, so do its challenges, and your ability to lead must evolve accordingly. This means expanding your power, developing new skills, and redefining your role.

Brian Chesky exemplifies how scaling personal leadership, adapting to challenges, and staying true to a mission can drive long-term success. As the co-founder and CEO of Airbnb, Chesky transformed a simple idea—renting out an air mattress in a San Francisco apartment—into a global platform that revolutionized the hospitality industry. His leadership centered on community empowerment, trust, and a vision of belonging, proving that scaling a business requires both innovation and a strong cultural foundation.

The result? Chesky's leadership fueled measurable business success:

- Scaled Airbnb from an idea in 2008 to a publicly traded company valued at over $100 billion (2021 IPO)

- Overcame the COVID-19 crisis by making tough but people-first decisions, including transparent layoffs and restructuring the business for long-term resilience

- Built a trust-based ecosystem with over 4 million hosts in over 220 countries, reshaping global travel and economic empowerment

Chesky's journey proves that personal growth at the top directly translates into business scalability.

Here's how you can apply the same approach to your leadership.

- **Expand Your Personal Power:** Your ability to lead with clarity and resilience defines the stability and success of your organization. Scaling your power matters because it:

  o Builds emotional resilience and helps you navigate setbacks while fostering a stable, high-performance culture

  o Transitions you from technician to strategist and enables you to focus on big-picture growth and long-term vision

  o Develops trust and empowerment and creates a culture of accountability, reducing reliance on you for every decision

  Scaling your leadership power means moving from managing operations to guiding a mission-driven company that thrives beyond your personal bandwidth.

- **Master the Skills That Bridge Vision and Execution:** Expanding your skill set ensures your leadership remains relevant as your company grows. Key leadership skills for scaling include:

  o Deep functional knowledge: Understanding the fundamentals of finance, marketing, and operations allows you to challenge, guide, and support your team effectively.

o Strategic agility: Leaders who invest in continuous learning can identify leverage points, adapt to trends, and avoid costly mistakes.

o Clear communication of vision: Scaling means ensuring that your entire team remains aligned, motivated, and connected to your mission.

- **Set the Tone for a Scalable Organization:** Your leadership style shapes your company's culture, and culture is what attracts and retains the right talent. Leadership sets the tone because:

    o Emotional intelligence plus accountability equals high-performing teams.

    o A resilient, mission-driven leader magnetizes top performers.

    o Your leadership determines if your team thrives or stagnates.

A purpose-driven CEO who grows personally can lead with greater clarity, foster a high-performing culture, and make decisions that drive long-term success.

We'll go deeper on how to scale yourself to scale your company in Part 2 – Step 3 of the book: "Scale yourself as a CEO."

STEP 4: SCALE YOUR TEAM PERFORMANCE

A high-performing, engaged team comes from scaling their power, skills, and roles, ensuring they have the autonomy, expertise, and clarity to drive the company's success.

Zappos exemplifies how empowering employees, fostering continuous learning, and defining purposeful roles create a world-class team. By adopting a self-managed structure like "Holacracy," employees own their decisions, trust is fostered, and collaboration thrives.

The result? Zappos' team-driven model delivered tangible business success:

- Seventy-five percent of its business comes from repeat customers, proving that engaged teams deliver consistent, exceptional service.

- It grew from almost no sales to over $1 billion in annual revenue within ten years, driven by word-of-mouth and customer loyalty.

- It ranked among the best in customer service, leading to its $1.2 billion acquisition by Amazon.

- It maintained only a 39 percent turnover in 2008, when the industry average for call centers was 150 percent, highlighting strong employee retention.

Zappos proves that scaling team performance is about structuring, empowering, and training them for long-term success. Here's how you can apply the same approach to your company.

- **Stop Micromanaging:** If you recruit people to tell them what to do, you will always have people waiting for you to tell them what to do. Scale leadership effectively by:

o Implementing cascading leadership: Ensure leadership values and behaviors are modeled and replicated across all levels.

o Building trust and reducing friction: Empowered teams work collaboratively, driving results without constant oversight.

o Enhancing agility: Teams with decision-making authority adapt quickly to challenges and opportunities.

o Strengthening mission alignment: Employees who own their work feel more connected to company goals.

• **Keep Them Learning (Strategically):** Skill development isn't about training for the sake of training; it's about investing in what truly drives performance. Keep learning effective by:

o Prioritizing quality over quantity: Focus on relevant, high-impact skills that drive business growth.

o Reducing unnecessary training costs: Targeted learning prevents wasteful spending on irrelevant programs.

o Enhancing retention and engagement: Employees who continuously grow stay longer, reducing turnover.

o Boosting adaptability and innovation: A learning culture ensures teams stay competitive in a rapidly changing market.

- **The Power of Specialists:** Scaling effectively means moving from generalist roles to specialized expertise, ensuring that every employee makes a targeted, high-value contribution. Specialization matters for scaling because it:

  - Reduces inefficiencies: Clearly defined roles streamline workflows, avoiding confusion and duplication.

  - Strengthens retention: Recognizing the value of all roles increases job satisfaction and loyalty.

  - Optimizes operational efficiency: Scaling without structured roles leads to bottlenecks and misalignment.

  - Enhances customer experience: Specialists can deliver excellence in their specific domain, increasing client retention.

We'll go deeper into how to scale your sustainable, high-performing team in Part 2 – Step 4 of the book: "Scale Your Team Performance."

STEP 5: SCALE YOUR ADAPTABILITY

When your business becomes adaptable, it becomes unstoppable because each failure becomes an opportunity to learn. However, if your business relies too heavily on you or key individuals, it becomes a bottleneck to scaling. Sustaining a high-performing business implies the following:

- Shifting from individual intelligence to collective intelligence

- Scaling the company's ability to measure, reflect, and iterate

- Ensuring the business can run without you, giving you also the freedom to exit at any time

As an example, Toyota exemplifies the power of scaling collective intelligence, fostering a culture where all employees actively collaborate to solve challenges through initiatives like "Waigaya" sessions, ensuring innovation and resilience. Its commitment to continuous improvement through "Kaizen" embeds iterative practices that balance short-term performance with long-term sustainability, keeping the company adaptable in a dynamic market.

The result? Toyota's adaptability delivered measurable business success:

- Operational excellence: Reduced production lead times by 50 percent and increased productivity by 20 percent through Kaizen and Waigaya sessions.

- Sustainability leadership: Sold over 15 million hybrid vehicles, reducing CO_2 emissions by over 120 million tons globally.

- Financial growth: Achieved record sales of 10.3 million vehicles in 2024, maintaining market leadership in a competitive industry.

Toyota proves that adaptability is about embedding resilience into the company's DNA. Here's how you can apply the same approach:

- **Harness Collective Intelligence:** Move from the power of the star to the power of the collective. A company that scales successfully leverages its entire team's intelligence rather than relying on a few key individuals. Collective intelligence drives adaptability by:

○ Decentralizing decision-making: Teams generate and execute solutions independently, ensuring agility in fast-changing environments.

○ Fostering innovation: A culture of collaboration leads to better problem-solving and continuous improvement.

○ Reducing dependency on key players: Ensures that growth and resilience aren't tied to any single leader.

○ Creating self-sufficient teams: Lightens the founder's operational burden, making the business scalable and sustainable.

When everyone contributes to problem-solving, the organization moves faster and adapts more efficiently.

- **Measure, Reflect, and Iterate:** Sustaining high performance requires a continuous cycle of measurement, reflection, and improvement. Iteration enhances adaptability by:

○ Balancing short-term wins with long-term excellence: Prevents burnout from rapid scaling while ensuring consistent growth.

○ Enhancing agility: Flexible goal-setting allows for rapid pivots when needed.

- o Driving operational efficiency: Aligning energy management with productivity cycles ensures peak performance.

- o Fueling innovation: A culture of feedback unlocks creativity and strategic problem-solving.

Embedding iterative processes keeps your team motivated, innovative, and prepared for long-term success.

- **Ability to Exit the Business:** A company that depends too much on its founder limits its potential. The key to true scalability is ensuring your company can operate independently of you. Founder independence strengthens the business by:

  - o Increasing investor confidence: A self-sustaining business is more scalable, resilient, and valuable.

  - o Enabling strategic focus: Founders can step back from daily operations to drive bigger initiatives. Enjoying life also brings fresh air to the business.

  - o Ensuring long-term impact: Embedding leadership development creates a lasting legacy.

We'll go deeper on how to scale your company's adaptability in Part 2 – Step 5 of the book: "Scale Your Adaptability."

By following these five steps, you'll scale your business in a way that builds lasting enterprise value, attracts strategic investors, and positions your company for exponential growth without burning out.

The compounded results will help you:

1. **Reclaim Your Time to Focus on High-Leverage Growth:** By reducing your involvement in daily operations, you gain the time and mental clarity to:

   - Lead at the highest level: Shift from operator to visionary, focusing on scaling strategies and long-term positioning.

   - Pursue game-changing opportunities: Explore new partnerships, funding rounds, or market expansions without being trapped in execution.

   - Strengthen your investor appeal: A business that can operate without its founder is significantly more attractive to VCs and strategic buyers.

   Imagine waking up each day inspired, knowing your company is thriving beyond your direct input, leaving you free to create, scale, and shape the industry.

2. **Build a Business That Gains Value Over Time**: A company built on autonomous leadership, mission alignment, and adaptability is a compounding asset that grows in value every year.

   - Increases valuation and investment potential: Businesses with scalable leadership and strong fundamentals attract growth-stage investors and impact VCs.

   - Ensures longevity and mission continuity: Your vision and impact continue even as leadership evolves or ownership transitions.

- Positions your company as a category leader: A well-structured company dominates its market and creates a lasting legacy.

Picture the sense of pride and fulfillment as your company scales beyond you, creating lasting impact, wealth, and industry influence.

3. **Strengthen Market Resilience and Investor Confidence:** By scaling with clarity, adaptability, and mission-driven execution, you'll build a company that thrives in any market condition.

   - Creates predictable, repeatable growth: Investors and stakeholders trust companies that demonstrate sustainable traction and execution discipline.

   - Reduces risk and increases stability: A resilient, high-performing team ensures business continuity, even in volatile markets.

   - Fosters stakeholder trust: A mission-driven, impact-aligned business earns loyalty from investors, customers, society, suppliers, and talent alike.

Imagine the confidence of knowing your company is built to outperform, no matter the challenges ahead.

4. **Keep Your Company at the Forefront of Innovation:** Companies that fail to evolve die, but those that embed a culture of innovation and adaptability stay ahead of the curve.

   - Empowers teams to solve challenges independently: Reduces reliance on the CEO for every decision, unlocking faster innovation cycles.

- Attracts new revenue opportunities: A highly adaptable company anticipates market shifts and monetizes emerging trends.

- Strengthens competitive positioning: Ensures your company remains a category leader with loyal customers and a reputation for excellence.

Imagine the competitive edge of knowing your team operates with focus, creativity, and precision, constantly refining, reinventing, and questioning boundaries.

5. **Scale Without Sacrificing Your Sanity:** Scaling shouldn't come at the cost of burnout. By stepping back from day-to-day execution and focusing on high-leverage leadership, you gain:

- Strategic clarity: Spend more time on vision, strategic partnerships, and capital allocation.

- Operational ease: Your company runs like a well-oiled machine without constant firefighting.

- Market dominance without exhaustion: Position yourself as an industry leader who scales with clarity rather than chaos.

Feel the profound relief of knowing your company is running smoothly, scaling intentionally, and fulfilling its purpose without sacrificing your energy or peace of mind.

Part 2 of the book will show you how to implement each step within your company, but before going there, let's take a step back to highlight the most important things in the book.

THE MOST IMPORTANT THINGS IN THIS BOOK

When you think about scaling your business, reconnect to your mission and market opportunity. The most investable, high-impact companies are those that align their mission with high-performance execution.

If you continue to invest in your leadership, your talent, and an iterative growth strategy, you won't just scale faster; you'll scale better than any short-term business trend could ever promise.

Now that we've dug into the myths and the main components of the approach, let me share with you how I help purpose-driven leaders scale their businesses in the most sustainable manner.

LEADING LIKE A HIGH-PERFORMANCE FOUNDER: SHARKS VS. DOLPHINS

There are two ways to lead an organization: the shark mindset or the dolphin mindset.

The Shark Mindset

Sharks are powerful, dominant, and aggressive. They operate in survival mode, always pushing forward, often alone. While their relentless drive may work in the short term, it is exhausting, isolating, and unsustainable.

- Sharks struggle to retain top talent: Employees feel like disposable assets rather than key contributors.
- Scaling is a constant battle: Growth depends entirely on the founder's force and control, creating bottlenecks.

- Investor confidence is lower: Businesses that rely too much on their CEO are considered high-risk investments.

The Dolphin Mindset
Dolphins, on the other hand, thrive in collaboration, adaptability, and intelligence. They move with purpose, attract allies, and create strong ecosystems that make them resilient.

- Dolphin leaders attract and retain top performers: People want to work for a company that fosters growth, autonomy, and purpose.

- Scaling becomes easier and more natural: The business operates on collective intelligence rather than individual control.

- Investors prioritize dolphin-led companies: Businesses with strong leadership, decentralized decision-making, and adaptability are considered prime investment opportunities.

If you want to build a business that attracts the best talent, scales sustainably, and is positioned for long-term success, leading as a dolphin is the way to go.

SCALING LIKE A SURFER: THE BILLION-DOLLAR PURPOSE APPROACH

Imagine your company as a surfer riding a wave. When you achieve market fit, it is like catching the perfect wave: You are aligned with the momentum, market demand, and investor interest.

The key to riding the waves of exponential growth is about learning to surf and have fun while being able to catch bigger and bigger waves.

The Billion-Dollar Purpose Approach ensures that:

- Your company remains agile, resilient, and capital-efficient.

- Your team operates at the highest level without dependency on you.

- Your scaling process is natural, sustainable, and investment-ready.

THE INVESTOR'S PERSPECTIVE: SURFERS VS. BOAT BUILDERS

Some founders try to "build a boat" to control the wave. They overhire, overload their operations, and burn through capital too quickly, only to collapse when the market shifts.

The best founders learn to "ride the wave."
They scale lean, focus on high-impact execution, and allow their mission and market forces to propel them forward naturally.

Investors bet on founders who can surf, not ones who sink their boats.

MY LONGER STORY

Although today I have found my purpose and am fully aligned with scaling mission-driven companies through conscious, high-performance strategies, it was not always like this.

For years, I thrived as a strategy consultant at top firms, working with Fortune 100 CEOs to shape and implement ambitious growth strategies. On the surface, we had all the right elements: bold visions, well-structured plans, and top-tier talent. In many ways, we achieved impressive results:

- Market expansion strategies delivered double-digit revenue growth.

- Operational transformations increased EBITDA margins.

- Innovative product launches secured first-mover advantages, capturing significant market share.

- Digital initiatives improved customer satisfaction scores, enhancing long-term retention.

Yet, despite these successes, many strategies failed to deliver lasting impact:

- Misalignment between leadership and teams caused ambitious plans to underperform.

- Burnout, lack of ownership, and siloed execution stalled implementation.

- High-performing teams struggled to sustain success, leading to costly turnover.

- Cultural resistance frequently derailed transformation, preventing real business shifts.

The root cause became increasingly clear: misalignment across the organization compounded by relentless burnout.

It wasn't just the organizations I was advising that were struggling; I, too, was living through burnout firsthand. For a long time, I believed that constantly pushing yourself was the only way to success. But the reality hit hard: That pace isn't sustainable.

I had to find another way.

THE LEADERSHIP SHIFT: FROM OVERWORKING TO SCALING SMARTER

This realization led me to mindfulness and psychology, which transformed my entire approach to leadership and business. I discovered that true success is not about doing more but about aligning with what truly matters. Ironically, I achieved more by doing less, something I had never thought possible before.

Then, life threw me one of the hardest challenges I'd ever faced: the loss of my child at birth through a medical termination of pregnancy. That loss reshaped me in ways I couldn't have anticipated. As devastating as it was, I found a strange kind of strength through it.

They say, "What doesn't kill you makes you stronger."

True strength does not come from denying pain. It comes from acknowledging it, living through it, and learning to rebuild. I often wonder: *Would the old me, the version that believed in relentless striving, have survived this?*

Out of that pain, I re-evaluated everything, including my career.

I launched my first company, Mindful Academy while working full-time, returning to school for psychology, and navigating the challenges of entrepreneurship. It was far harder than I expected, but it forced me to focus on what truly mattered: trust, resilience, and clarity.

During this time, I also became a mother again. It was a reminder that success is meaningless if it comes at the cost of what truly matters.

With these lessons, I made a bold move: I left my corporate job and relocated to my home country. It was a leap of faith: an opportunity to give my family a more fulfilling environment, surrounded by loved ones, under the sun, next to the waves.

At the same time, I continued refining a new, more sustainable business scaling methodology: testing, adapting, and improving it until I saw measurable, repeatable success.

From Personal Growth to Scalable Business Impact

As I refined and implemented my approach, my clients saw transformative results:

- Employee retention and engagement significantly improved, leading to higher profitability and lower operational costs.

- Leadership became more aligned, enabling faster, more efficient decision-making and reducing bottlenecks.

- Companies scaled with increased profitability and valuation, making them prime investment opportunities.

- Organizations became more resilient to market shifts, ensuring long-term growth and adaptability.

One of the most unexpected lessons came from surfing. What began as a personal escape became an unexpected business coaching tool. Surfing taught me that life and business could be simpler: You can flow with the waves, stay focused, and find joy in the process.

This insight reinforced the Billion-Dollar Purpose Approach, an integration of strategic advisory, mindfulness, entrepreneurship, surfing, and leadership into a scalable, investment-ready growth framework.

THE BILLION-DOLLAR PURPOSE APPROACH WORKS

Purpose-driven leaders working with me so far reported:

- Achieving scalable growth while preserving their mission, values, and company culture

- Transformational leadership shifts, resulting in autonomous, high-performing teams that drive innovation

- Stronger financial resilience and adaptability, ensuring they outperform in dynamic market conditions

- A blend of business success and personal fulfillment, creating a sustainable work-life balance

This approach is about building a scalable, high-value enterprise that thrives at scale.

Let's ride the waves!

PART 2

HOW TO SCALE YOUR BILLION-DOLLAR PURPOSE

STEP 1:
SCALE YOUR MISSION

SUMMARY

Scaling your mission is the key to aligning your company's growth with your evolving purpose, ensuring that every decision and action amplifies your impact. This chapter provides a step-by-step approach to achieving sustainable growth while maintaining strategic clarity, stakeholder alignment, and operational focus.

Scaling your mission is structured into three actionable strategies:

1. **Evolve Your Mission:** Unlock a higher, more impactful version of your mission that reflects your company's current reality and future aspirations. By redefining your mission as your business scales, you will build a dynamic, mission-driven roadmap that re-engages your team, attracts top talent, and creates alignment across all areas of your business.

2. **Engage Your Stakeholders:** Align your strategy with your market's evolving needs and expectations to create a deeply informed, stakeholder-driven approach. By actively listening to investors, customers, employees,

and partners, you will foster trust, loyalty, and long-term scalability while making data-backed decisions that drive intentional growth.

3. **Get Clarity on Your Focus Areas:** Avoid the trap of trying to scale everything at once. Instead, build a focused scaling strategy that prioritizes leverage points, optimizes resources, and drives exponential growth, all while maintaining alignment with your mission.

Together, these three strategies provide a clear, actionable framework for scaling your business with clarity, intention, and purpose. By implementing them, you will ensure that your company not only grows but also thrives by delivering lasting impact while staying true to its core values.

Let's dive into how to implement each.

EVOLVE YOUR MISSION: HOW YOUR MISSION EVOLVES AND WHY LEADERS MUST ACKNOWLEDGE IT

Many leaders who have achieved mission-driven success tell me, "I feel like we've moved away from our mission." But this is a limited belief. The notion that as your company grows, you drift away from your mission is based on the misunderstanding that a mission doesn't evolve. The truth is, as your company expands, your mission grows with you.

HOW MY MISSION EVOLVED

Seven years ago, I began a personal transformation, and mindfulness helped me overcome the challenges I was facing both personally and professionally. After a professional burnout, I sought solutions and found a mindfulness teacher and a therapist who guided me. The results fascinated me and sparked my curiosity, leading me to delve deeper into psychology and mindfulness.

Just when I thought I had gone through the hardest period of my life, I faced the loss of a child at birth through a medical termination of pregnancy. It was, and still is, the most painful experience of my life. However, because of the mindfulness training I had undergone, I felt I was able to cope in a way that the old me couldn't have. This propelled me into teaching mindfulness as a side hustle. At that time, my mission was to help people become stronger in the face of adversity by elevating their consciousness through mindfulness training. I coached individuals, offered courses, and eventually shifted online when the pandemic hit.

As I helped people, I noticed that many of their struggles stemmed from their professional lives. I felt a calling to address the issues within companies. As my consciousness evolved, I began to see the harm that unconscious business practices were doing to people and the planet. I realized that my mission wasn't just to teach mindfulness; it was to bridge mindfulness and strategy consulting, helping purpose-driven companies scale sustainably and profitably. In doing so, I contribute to the well-being of both people and the planet.

The more purpose-driven companies we have, and the more they scale, the more we put resources into the hands of those with positive intentions. This creates purpose-driven, fulfilling jobs and solutions that respect the planet.

It's a win-win-win.

My original mission allowed me to make initial strides, achieve results, and feel satisfaction. However, as I scaled my mission, I felt a new calling. I asked myself, "What's the next step?" If I had forced myself to stick to my original mission, I never would have launched this new offering, which combines my over twelve years of strategy consulting and over five years of mindfulness and psychology. I wouldn't have written this book, and you wouldn't be reading it now.

This evolution of mission is not unique to me. Many purpose-driven companies have gone through similar transformations.

CASE STUDY:
PATAGONIA, SCALING WITH PURPOSE

When Yvon Chouinard founded Patagonia in 1973, its mission was primarily to create high-quality outdoor clothing and gear for climbers. However, as Patagonia grew, so did its understanding of its role in environmental stewardship.

Today, Patagonia's mission has evolved to a much broader and impactful purpose:

"We're in business to save our home planet."

This mission now focuses on environmental activism and sustainability, allowing the company to scale while aligning with its evolving values and contributing positively to the planet. Patagonia's evolving mission became a powerful force that attracted like-minded customers and top talent who were passionate about environmental causes.

SCALING REQUIRES MISSION EVOLUTION

When something bigger seems to be calling you, I invite you to listen and bring it into the driver's seat.

This process of discovery isn't about going back to square one. It's about creating a new reality that aligns with the current stage of your life and business. Think of it like moving up a spiral. While you may feel like you're facing the same challenges or reflections, you're actually at a higher level, looking at things from a more advanced perspective.

The person you are today and the company you've built have gone through many cycles of growth. When you embrace the higher-level mission that aligns with your present and future, you align your energy in service to your current reality and aspirations, which gives fuel and strength to your scaling process.

THE IMPORTANCE OF REGULARLY REASSESSING YOUR MISSION

Similarly, when I start working with a new client, I never assume I know their mission or that their mission today is the same as when they first started. I don't believe there is one fixed way to define a mission, nor do I expect companies to stick to what they initially thought their mission was. Instead, I guide them through a process of discovery to explore who they are now and where they are now. Is it still the same calling? Is it a bigger calling?

One of the reasons many companies struggle to scale is because they focus on returning to the past, staying stuck to their original mission even when their heart and intuition invite them to consider more. These fears of change can cause a company failure or limited growth.

WHAT HAPPENS WHEN COMPANIES RESIST MISSION EVOLUTION?

When a company clings to a mission that no longer aligns with its current reality, misalignment spreads across the organization.

- Loss of top talent: High-performers seek meaningful work. If your mission feels outdated or disconnected, they leave.

- Investor hesitation: Investors look for companies that evolve with market needs. A stagnant mission makes a business look rigid and high-risk.

- Slowed innovation and growth: Businesses anchored in past objectives struggle to pivot, adapt, and seize new opportunities.

Conversely, companies that proactively evolve their mission build alignment, attract high-performing talent, and sustain long-term impact.

FIVE STEPS TO REASSESS AND ALIGN YOUR MISSION

1. Engage in Mission Discovery

    - Take a step back. What are the core values driving your decisions today?

    - What challenges and opportunities exist now that weren't there before?

    - How have you and your company changed? What drives your passion today?

Your mission isn't what it was; it's what it needs to be now.

2. Involve Your Leadership Team

    - Ask your leadership team: "What do you believe our company's current mission is?"

    - Are our daily actions and decisions aligned with this mission?

    - Are we holding onto old ideas out of habit, even when our work suggests otherwise?

Mission evolution must be a collective realization, not just a top-down decision.

3. Define Your Present Mission

    - Clearly articulate your mission today, not what it was when you started.

    - Ensure it aligns with your current growth, values, and goals.

- Ask, "Does this mission still feel relevant, inspiring, and aligned with where we're headed?"

This process isn't about changing for the sake of change; it's about recognizing what already evolved and defining it with clarity.

4. Communicate Your New Mission Clearly

- Ensure every team member understands and connects with your evolved mission.

- Mission clarity attracts aligned high-performing talent and strengthens retention.

- For those who no longer resonate with the mission, this is their opportunity to leave.

A mission isn't just words on a website; it's the heartbeat of company culture.

5. Commit to Ongoing Evaluation

- Regularly check that your mission is still aligned with your company's growth.

- If not, adjust. The most impactful companies evolve their mission before it feels outdated.

Your mission should be a living, evolving force, not a fixed statement from the past.

PUT YOUR EVOLVING MISSION IN THE DRIVER'S SEAT

Imagine your mission as the driving force behind your company's success, guiding your strategy, attracting high-performing talent, and shaping the future of your industry.

The most impactful leaders don't define their mission once and never revisit it. They continuously evolve it, aligning it with their present reality and future ambitions.

Your mission isn't just your starting point. It's your scaling strategy.

So, ask yourself if your mission is aligned with your next stage of growth.

Then, confront that with the voice of your stakeholders. This is what we will tackle in the next chapter.

JUST ASK: COLLECT THE VOICE OF YOUR STAKEHOLDERS

The phrase that will keep you stuck in the past and prevent you from scaling is:
"I already know that."

The mindset that will unlock your next level of growth is:
"Tell me more about it."

Founders and investors often make decisions based on past successes, internal assumptions, or instincts, but true scaling requires something more: a continuous feedback loop with your stakeholders.

If you want to build a billion-dollar company with purpose, you need to take stock of where you actually stand, not where you *assume* you stand. The best founders don't scale alone; they listen, iterate, and adapt based on real-time insights from the people who matter most to their business.

WHY YOU MUST TAKE STOCK WHILE SCALING

Scaling without data from your environment is like sailing without a compass. Without a comprehensive awareness of where you are, your strategies are based on assumptions leading to random, reactive decisions rather than deliberate, scalable growth.

- Do you want to attract investment at the right valuation? You need to understand what investors see in your business and where they see risk.

- Do you want to accelerate revenue growth? You need to know why customers buy, why they leave, and what would make them stay.

- Do you want to retain top talent? You need to understand what truly motivates them and what might drive them away.

Too many founders operate in guesswork mode rather than feedback mode, but the fastest way to remove blind spots and accelerate growth is simple:

Just ask.

THE POWER OF ASKING: A SIMPLE APPROACH TO SCALING

Early in my career as a strategy consultant, I spent countless hours building complex business cases with extensive research, hoping to provide the best possible recommendations. Yet, I often found myself wondering, *Am I missing something? Am I an imposter?*

I sought advice from mentors. Some told me to work on my self-confidence. Others advised me to conduct deeper market research. I tried both:

- I hired a coach who gave me the advice: "Leïla, walk like a queen!" While amusing, it didn't make me a better consultant.

- I gathered more data, but many reports were outdated, biased, or irrelevant to the business context I was working in.

Then, I discovered a much simpler and more powerful approach.

I started asking the right people the right questions.

I went directly to executives, investors, customers, and employees and asked:

- "What do you see as the biggest opportunity?"

- "What concerns you most about the future?"

- "What do you wish we had done differently?"

The insights I gained completely changed the quality of my recommendations and the same applies to scaling a company. Instead of making assumptions about what investors, customers, or employees want, simply ask them.

The Five Stakeholder Groups You Must Engage to Scale

If you want to build a profitable, purpose-driven company at scale, these are the five key stakeholder groups whose voices you must collect:

1. **Investors** → *Want them to keep investing?* Ask what they need to see for continued confidence.

2. **Customers** → *Want to retain and expand your client base?* Ask what makes them stay and what could make them leave.

3. **Suppliers and Partners** → *Want long-term collaboration?* Ask what keeps them loyal and where they see risk.

4. **Public and Brand Perception** → *Want your brand to be an asset?* Assess how the public perceives your impact and credibility.

5. **Talent and Leadership Team** → *Want to keep your best people?* Ask what makes them engaged and what could make them leave.

These five areas determine the trajectory of your business. If you consistently gather, analyze, and act on stakeholder feedback, you will outperform competitors who operate on assumptions.

THE BILLION-DOLLAR QUESTION: WHAT HAPPENS WHEN YOU TRULY LISTEN?

When you build a feedback-driven organization, the results speak for themselves:

- Engaged investors keep investing.
- Loyal customers keep buying.
- Strong supplier relationships lead to better service and costs.
- A respected brand attracts more opportunities.

- High-performing talent creates solutions before problems arise.

This is the foundation of sustainable, scalable business success.

Just as I mentioned in the surfing metaphor in the first part of the book, scaling effectively isn't about forcing things or overloading the system. It's about aligning with the natural flow, adjusting to the feedback from all stakeholders, and riding the wave smoothly toward sustainable growth.

CASE STUDIES: HOW LEADING COMPANIES SCALED BY ENGAGING STAKEHOLDERS

The best companies don't just build products; they build relationships.

- Airbnb: Listening to Hosts and Communities to Scale Sustainably

Airbnb realized that scaling isn't just about guests; it's also about hosts and communities. To strengthen its ecosystem, the company established a Host Advisory Board to collect direct feedback from hosts, ensuring that its policies and platform improvements benefited both sides of its marketplace.

By also engaging with local communities and regulators, Airbnb was able to expand globally while avoiding the backlash that many tech platforms face.

- LEGO: Rebuilding by Listening to Fans and Employees

LEGO nearly collapsed in the early 2000s due to internal misalignment and poor strategic decisions. The company turned things around by implementing LEGO Ideas, a platform where fans submit product concepts. It also actively involved employees and suppliers in the innovation process.

By making stakeholder input the core of its strategy, LEGO not only rebounded but also became one of the world's most valuable brands.

Scaling Through Stakeholder Intelligence

Imagine scaling your company not through guesswork but by leveraging the insights of those who care most about its success.

- Instead of hoping investors stay on board, engage them proactively.
- Instead of guessing what customers want, listen deeply.
- Instead of losing top talent, ask what will keep them committed.

What if your next billion-dollar decision was just one conversation away?

The Next Step: Make Stakeholder Feedback a Habit

The best founders and investors don't just collect feedback once; they embed it into their culture.

- **Regular investor check-ins** ensure alignment with the scaling strategy.
- **Customer listening sessions** reveal shifting preferences before competitors notice.

- **Quarterly talent assessments** prevent leadership blind spots and disengagement.

By systematically gathering and acting on feedback, you future-proof the scaling of your business.

Are You Ready to Ask the Right Questions?

The fastest-growing purpose-driven companies don't operate in isolation. They succeed by building businesses with their stakeholders, not just for them.

So ask yourself:

- *What key insights am I missing by not engaging my stakeholders?*

- *How would my company scale faster if I collected and acted on real-time feedback?*

- *What's one question I can ask today that could unlock my next level of growth?*

A billion-dollar purpose isn't built in a vacuum.

It's built through conversations that matter.

From Clarity to Focus: The Key to Scaling with Precision

In the previous chapters, we explored two critical components of sustainable growth:

1. **Scaling Your Mission with Intention**: Understanding that your mission must evolve as your company grows,

ensuring your purpose aligns with the reality of your business today.

2. **Listening to the Voice of Your Stakeholders**: Collecting insights from investors, customers, talent, and partners to remove blind spots and make informed, high-impact decisions.

These steps give you clarity, but clarity alone isn't enough.

Many founders and investors fail not because they lack vision but because they try to do too much at once.

Scaling requires focus.

The next step is knowing where to allocate your resources, energy, and leadership attention to drive exponential, sustainable growth. Scaling isn't about chasing every opportunity; it's about choosing the right battles and executing them with precision.

Get Clarity on Your Areas of Focus

Scaling is about doing the right things exceptionally well. It's the ultimate scaling advantage.

The biggest mistake I see purpose-driven founders make after raising funding is trying to fix everything at once. They hire rapidly, expand into new initiatives, and spread resources across too many priorities only to find themselves stuck in inefficiency, talent churn, and stalled growth.

The Pareto Principle tells us that 80 percent of results come from just 20 percent of actions. In scaling talent, impact, and revenue, this rule becomes even more critical. Your job as a founder or investor is to identify and double down on the few areas that create the greatest leverage rather than try to fix everything at the same time.

WHY TRYING TO FIX EVERYTHING WON'T WORK

After conducting a stakeholder assessment and refining your mission, it's tempting to say:
"Let's hire aggressively and solve all our challenges at once!"

However, hiring without focus leads to:

- Confused priorities: Teams working on disconnected efforts with no clear impact.

- Bloated operations: High overhead without strategic alignment.

- Burnout and disengagement: Employees spread too thin across non-essential tasks.

Instead of chasing everything, take a step back and ask: "What are the fewest things we need to get right to scale exponentially?"

FIND YOUR LEVERAGE POINTS: SCALING LIKE SLACK

The best companies don't scale by doing more; they scale by doing the essential things better than anyone else.

Take Slack as an example. When Slack was scaling, it didn't try to build an all-in-one enterprise suite or expand into unrelated markets. Instead, they focused on solving one core problem: team communication.

- They refined their product based on user feedback.

- They doubled down on seamless integrations.

- They ensured a frictionless onboarding experience.

By maintaining this clarity and discipline, Slack scaled into a dominant SaaS powerhouse without overextending or diluting its mission.

THE COST OF UNFOCUSED HIRING: AVOID THESE TRAPS

Some of the biggest mistakes in scaling are hiring too soon, too broadly, or without strategic clarity. Founders often believe hiring will solve their challenges, but they end up making one of three common mistakes:

1. Unclear task: If you don't know what needs to be done, how can you expect a new hire to know?

2. Lack of expertise: If you don't understand the role well enough to define success, how will you measure performance?

3. Low-priority work: If the task isn't critical to your leverage points, why are you hiring for it?

Hiring without clarity results in misalignment, wasted resources, and frustration. Instead of rushing to recruit, step back and ask:

- Is this hire solving a core problem?

- Do I have a clear success metric for this role?

- Will this role create a ripple effect of positive impact?

If the answer to any of these is no, pause and reassess before making a costly mistake.

SCALING BY FOCUS: HOW NETFLIX DOMINATED THE STREAMING INDUSTRY

Netflix didn't become a global leader by trying to do everything at once.

When transitioning from DVD rentals to streaming, they made a critical strategic choice:

- Instead of splitting focus between DVDs and digital, they went all-in on streaming.

- They built technology, content licensing, and a user experience optimized for this shift.

- They resisted distractions like gaming, hardware, or unrelated entertainment services.

By prioritizing its leverage point—on-demand content— Netflix scaled efficiently.

However, what happens when a company tries to do too much without a clear focus?

WeWork: A Masterclass in Overextension

WeWork didn't fail because co-working wasn't a viable business. It failed because it lost focus.

Instead of scaling a profitable, operationally sound workspace business, WeWork:

- Expanded into education (WeGrow), residential (WeLive), and event spaces without validating profitability

- Hired aggressively without clear financial sustainability

- Over-leveraged on long-term leases, assuming infinite growth

The results were a failed IPO, billions lost, and a business model collapse.

Quibi: A Billion-Dollar Lesson in Misplaced Priorities

Quibi raised $1.75 billion in funding to revolutionize short-form mobile streaming, but within six months, it failed.

Why?

- It rushed into production without testing market demand.

- It assumed people wanted Hollywood-quality content on mobile but never validated the need.

- It invested in celebrity-backed shows instead of customer-driven insights.

What's the lesson? Funding doesn't replace strategic clarity. Without focus, even billions in investment won't save you.

How to Identify Your Scaling Priorities: The Chain of Causality Method

Instead of reactively fixing problems, identify which single leverage point unlocks the most impact using this method:

1. List your challenges: Brainstorm everything slowing your business down.

2. Ask: "If I solve this, what other problems improve automatically?"

3. Follow the chain: Keep going until you find the root issue that drives everything else.

Example:

- Low customer retention → Caused by poor onboarding

- Poor onboarding → Due to unclear customer education

- Unclear customer education → Because marketing is misaligned with user expectations

Solution: Instead of hiring across sales, support, and product all at once, fix marketing clarity first, and other issues improve.

FOCUS FIRST, SCALE SMARTER

The stories of Slack and Netflix show us that strategic focus fuels sustainable growth. The failures of WeWork and Quibi highlight the risks of scattered expansion and lack of clarity.

Before you scale, ask yourself:

- What is the *one* thing we must get right to unlock growth?

- If we solve this, what other challenges will be resolved naturally?

- Are we hiring for strategic leverage or just for workload relief?

When you have absolute clarity on your mission and scaling priorities, your hiring, product strategy, and execution align for maximum impact.

Next Steps: From Focus to Execution

Clarity isn't just about knowing what to do; it's about ensuring your team is built to execute it effectively.

That's why I created a step-by-step cheat sheet that will help you:

- Identify your highest-leverage focus areas
- Avoid the most common hiring mistakes
- Build a roadmap for sustainable, strategic growth

Download it now: leilalahbabi.com/impactatscalecheatsheets

Once you have clarity on your focus, the next step is ensuring you attract and retain the right talent to execute it with precision.

STEP 2:
SCALE YOUR TALENT ATTRACTION AND RETENTION

Summary

Successfully scaling your company isn't just about increasing headcount; it's about ensuring every hire strengthens your mission, fuels long-term impact, and contributes to a thriving, values-driven culture. This chapter provides a step-by-step approach to attracting, integrating, and retaining top talent who will propel your organization forward with purpose and precision.

Scaling your talent strategy is structured into three actionable strategies:

1. **Attract and Retain Mission-Aligned Talent:** Build a resilient workforce by identifying and engaging individuals who align with your company's purpose. By prioritizing values-driven hiring and strategic retention, you will reduce turnover, enhance employee satisfaction, and create a foundation for sustainable growth.

2. **Cultivate a Magnetic Culture:** Develop an environment that naturally draws in high-performing leaders

and contributors who are deeply connected to your mission. By fostering engagement, innovation, and team alignment, you will create a workplace where top talent stays and thrives.

3. **Optimize Onboarding and Integration:** Ensure new hires become impactful contributors quickly by implementing seamless onboarding processes. A structured approach accelerates productivity, minimizes costly hiring mistakes, and embeds new employees into your company's mission from day one.

Together, these three strategies provide a clear, actionable framework for scaling your business with the right people, culture, and processes. By implementing them, you will not only grow your company but also amplify its impact by cultivating a team that is fully invested in your mission.

Let's dive into how to implement each.

RETENTION: THE OVERLOOKED SCALING STRATEGY AND WHY RETENTION MATTERS MORE THAN RECRUITMENT

The success of any company ultimately hinges on its people. Yet, in today's fast-paced, competitive world, the tenure of talent has drastically shortened, with the average talent staying just two years.

The cost of recruitment is high, estimated at half a year's salary, and the process of getting new hires up to speed can take another six months in addition to the time required to find the right person.

During this time, the company isn't operating at full efficiency, losing both the value of that role and overall operational effectiveness.

However, it's not just about the upfront costs of recruitment. Long-term retention of the right talent leads to the accumulation of deep institutional knowledge. Top talent becomes increasingly valuable, not just through efficiency but by driving the company's growth with their insights, innovation, and contributions to continuous improvement.

Without retaining this key talent, a company risks losing more than just productivity. It loses the potential for long-term innovation and sustainable growth.

With these stakes, it's clear that companies that chase talent in an endless cycle of recruiting, onboarding, and turnover are trapped in a losing game. This cycle drains resources, both financial and emotional, making it harder to scale and deliver on long-term goals.

Companies Winning Through Retention

Some of the most resilient, mission-driven companies have cracked the retention code.

- **Patagonia:** With a 4 percent turnover rate, Patagonia has mastered values-based retention by aligning its workplace culture with employees who deeply believe in its mission.

- **Ben & Jerry's:** Known for its low employee churn, the company attracts and retains talent through authentic leadership, social responsibility, and purpose-driven incentives.

The lesson is clear: Retention is a competitive advantage, but only when focused on keeping the right people.

Keeping the Right People

Retention isn't about keeping everyone; it's about keeping the right people. By the right people, I mean the high performers who are aligned with your company's mission and goals. The quality of retention matters more than the quantity. When you focus on engaging and motivating your top talent, you build a strong foundation for long-term success.

Here's what effective retention looks like in practice:

- **Long-Term Satisfaction and Cultural Fit**:
  - Top talent stays because they are genuinely engaged, see growth opportunities, and resonate with the company's values.

- o The right talent stays because they are genuinely satisfied with their jobs, feel challenged, and see opportunities for growth. They feel like integral parts of its mission, leading to higher motivation, stronger commitment, and better results.

- **Growth and Challenge**:

  - o Top talent doesn't just want a random job; they are eager to grow. When they have clear paths for advancement and opportunities to expand their skills and feel challenged, they stay.

  - o Effective retention focuses on keeping this key talent engaged by ensuring they have room to grow and develop within the company.

A strong retention culture creates operational efficiency, continuous innovation, and a team deeply invested in the company's future.

UNDERSTAND WHAT YOUR TALENT VALUES MOST

The key to building lasting retention isn't about replicating strategies from other companies or following market trends. Don't waste your time and energy there. What truly matters is understanding what your talent values most and offering them what genuinely resonates with their values.

As I explained earlier in the book with the boat and surf metaphor, trying to apply generic, market-driven retention strategies is like building a boat—heavy, rigid, and often ineffective. For example, offering perks like unlimited vacation days or trendy office spaces may seem appealing, but if these don't align with what your talent truly values, they become empty benefits that do little for long-term retention. These "boat" strategies create unnecessary complexity without delivering real results.

On the other hand, asking your talent what they want and responding to those requests is like surfing the wave in a natural, fluid, and far more sustainable way. When you build your retention strategy based on direct feedback, it becomes tailored to your people and your company culture, leading to deeper loyalty and long-term success.

ASK THE RIGHT QUESTIONS

When you ask the right questions and open a genuine dialogue with your talent, you ride the wave. This shows that you're invested in understanding their personal and professional aspirations. Some key questions to guide these conversations:

- What motivates you most in your work?
- What aspects of your job make you feel most engaged?
- What would make you want to stay here long-term?

The answers to these questions will help you uncover what your talent truly values, whether it's flexibility, growth opportunities, a sense of purpose, or recognition. This approach allows you to craft a retention strategy that fits your people and your business.

RETENTION STARTS WITH THE FOUNDER'S VALUES

A critical but often overlooked factor in retention is the founder's values and leadership approach.

The key insights I've discovered when working with founders are:

- The people who stay long-term are often those who share the founder's core values.

- Before defining a retention strategy, founders must first get crystal clear on what they value most in work and leadership.

A Simple Retention Exercise for Founders

1. Define your core values: What do you personally value most in your work?

2. Identify alignment: Do the people on your team share these values?

3. Tailor your retention strategy: Retain employees who thrive in your culture rather than just offering generic perks.

The more aligned your leadership approach is with your team's values, the stronger your retention will be.

Retention Is the Ultimate Competitive Advantage

Imagine if, instead of constantly chasing new talent, you could build a culture that attracts the right people organically.

Retention isn't just about keeping people; it's about creating an environment where high performers want to stay and contribute long-term.

The Business Case for Retention Over Recruitment

While competitors struggle with:

- High turnover
- Constant rehiring cycles
- Soaring recruitment costs

Your company could be running smoothly with a committed, mission-driven team, reducing churn, maintaining institutional knowledge, and scaling without unnecessary friction.

A strong retention strategy ensures that:

- Your company continuously evolves with the same trusted team.
- Your brand becomes a magnet for the right talent.
- Your resources go into growth, not endless hiring.

Final Thought: If You're Not Sure, Just Ask

The simplest way to build a strong retention culture is to start by listening.

- Ask your team what they value.
- Align your retention strategy with your mission.
- Keep the right people who will scale with you.

Retention isn't just an HR metric but a scalability strategy.

It starts with understanding what truly keeps high performers engaged, fulfilled, and committed to your company's vision.

How To Build Your Brand and Culture (Why Values Matter for Business Success)

"People will forget what you said, people will forget what you did, but people will never forget how you made them feel."

—Maya Angelou

This is the essence of company culture.

Many founders think of values as trendy buzzwords to use for employer branding. However, values are more than words on a website. They are how your company operates daily, how decisions are made, and how people experience your brand.

Companies that live their values build:

- Stronger brand loyalty among customers
- Higher engagement and retention among employees
- A culture of trust, innovation, and long-term success

Lived values are a key driven of a sustainable financial performance.

The ROI of Living Your Values

Companies with strong, well-defined cultures experience:

- Four times higher revenue growth than companies with weak cultures *(Harvard Business Review, Forbes)*
- Thirty-one percent lower voluntary turnover rates when they have strong employee recognition programs *(Select Software Reviews)*

95

- Higher employee engagement, which leads to greater profitability, lower absenteeism, and increased retention *(Gallup Research on Employee Engagement)*

Values-driven companies create an environment where people want to stay and contribute long-term.

WHAT "LIVING" VALUES ACTUALLY MEANS

Values guide everything we do. They inform decision-making, influence behavior, and shape how we interact with customers, talent, and partners. Values aren't just about what we do; they're about *how* we do it.

I'll never forget the time I walked into a luxury store in Paris as a student. Despite the elegance of the store, two salespeople exchanged glances, and one said, "I choose my customers." I immediately felt unwelcome and vowed never to buy from that brand, even when I could afford it.

That experience wasn't about the product; it was about the values expressed in that moment. Every interaction—no matter how small—reflects your company's values; make sure it cascades through your organization correctly. Values are lived in every action and interaction, and they have a profound effect on how your brand is perceived.

How to Build "Living" Values

So, how do you build values that are more than just words on a wall—values that are authentically lived and felt throughout your company? There are two key approaches:

1. Inside-Out: Start with You, the Founder

In the early days, your company is an extension of you. You hire based on intuition. You attract people who "just get it." However, as you scale, relying on instinct alone doesn't work.

Without clearly defined values, your culture starts to dilute. Misalignment creeps in. Decision-making becomes inconsistent.

This is why founders must define their core values intentionally before scaling.

- When values are clear, they create a shared compass: Your team can make decisions that align with your mission, even without your direct involvement.

- Your company becomes magnetic: You naturally attract employees, clients, and partners who resonate with your mission.

- Your business scales without losing its identity: Your team upholds your values at every stage of growth.

This is the power of intentionality in action.

I remember sitting across from a psychologist who asked me: "What words do you find yourself repeating most often?"

At first, I didn't know. However, as we went through my notes, patterns emerged. I ranked these recurring words and uncovered my true core values, the ones that had unconsciously driven my decisions for years.

It was a revelation. I could finally see the "why" behind so much of what I had done and felt.

For founders, this introspection is essential. Your values already shape your company, but when you uncover them consciously, they become a powerful foundation for growth.

When values are scaled across your organization, they protect the soul of your company. You don't have to worry about losing what makes your business unique. Instead, your team takes ownership of these values, embedding them into every decision.

This is about scaling your business by scaling yourself.

Your clarity becomes their clarity. Your passion becomes their passion.

2. Outside-In: Engage with Stakeholders

While introspection is crucial, founders must also assess how their values are actually perceived.

Companies often claim values that don't match reality. This is where stakeholder feedback becomes invaluable.

When I conduct this analysis with my clients, I ask open-ended questions to uncover:

- What do employees believe the company truly stands for?
- What values do customers experience when interacting with the brand?
- Where is the gap between stated values and lived values?

CASE STUDY: VALUES IN ACTION – A PERSONAL EXAMPLE

I once asked my father why he stayed at the same company for 45 years and why so many of his colleagues did the same.

His answer was simple: "Respect, collective responsibility, and care."

"When someone makes a mistake," he told me, "we don't point fingers. We take collective responsibility and help each other. It's never about individual performance; it's about the collective."

These values weren't written on a wall; they were lived daily.

The company thrived through economic ups and downs not because of a brilliant strategy but because its people felt valued and respected.

CASE STUDY: SALESFORCE – SCALING WITH STRONG VALUES

Salesforce is one of the most successful SaaS companies, not just because of its technology but because of its values.

Their core values—trust, customer success, innovation, and equality—are more than marketing statements. They shape every aspect of company culture and decision-making:

- The company integrates equality and inclusivity into its hiring and leadership structures.

- Salesforce consistently ranks as one of the best places to work, attracting and retaining top talent.

- Employees report higher job satisfaction because they feel aligned with the company's values and purpose.

By embedding these values into its culture, Salesforce scaled into a multi-billion-dollar company without losing its identity.

WHAT IF YOUR COMPANY TRULY LIVED ITS VALUES?

What if every employee, from entry-level to leadership, was fully aligned with your mission and lived your values daily?

When values are authentic, your employees naturally become ambassadors of your brand.

This leads to:

- Higher engagement
- Lower turnover
- A thriving, purpose-driven company

Founders who build a culture of living values scale their businesses and scale movements.

Once your company's culture is deeply aligned with your values, attracting and onboarding the right fit becomes significantly easier. The next chapter focuses on how to maximize your chances of successfully attracting and onboarding the right talent, ensuring that every new hire strengthens, not dilutes, your company's mission and culture.

WHY HIRING THE RIGHT FIT MATTERS MORE THAN JUST SKILLS

Most companies fail at scaling not because they can't find talent but because they hire the wrong people for the wrong reasons.

A common mistake companies make in recruitment is believing that scaling requires hiring the most skilled people and offering the highest salaries. While skills and compensation are important, hiring solely based on these factors can lead to high turnover and costly mistakes. Candidates who join for the paycheck often leave for a better offer elsewhere. To scale effectively, you need to focus on attracting talent who believe in your company's mission and align with your values.

The right fit is not just about technical skills or impressive credentials; it's about finding individuals who resonate with your purpose and long-term vision. This approach helps build a committed, purpose-driven workforce that contributes to sustainable growth.

WHAT IT MEANS TO FIND THE RIGHT FIT

Many founders assume that the right fit means hiring the most impressive candidate on paper. But that's a dangerous misconception.

- Right fit ≠ highest-performing candidate based on resume
- Right fit = someone who aligns with your company's mission, thrives in your culture, and is committed to growing with you

When you have clarity on your company's mission and values, hiring decisions become easier and more strategic. Instead of bringing in someone who looks good on paper but doesn't align culturally, you attract people who will thrive in your environment.

DATA-DRIVEN PROOF: WHY CULTURAL FIT MATTERS

- Companies that prioritize culture and mission out-perform competitors by 202 percent in profitability *(Harvard Business Review, Forbes).*

- Seventy-two percent of candidates consider company culture before accepting a job offer *(Glassdoor).*

What this means:
Offering the highest salary alone won't necessarily attract the right talent. People who come for money will leave for money. Instead, you need candidates who resonate with your long-term vision, leading to a more engaged, loyal, and high-performing team.

CASE STUDY: SALESFORCE – PURPOSE AND COMPENSATION IN ACTION

Salesforce provides a strong example of a company that effectively blends purpose with fair compensation. Known for its commitment to trust, equality, and customer success, Salesforce encourages its talent to engage in social good through its 1-1-1 model—donating 1 percent of its product, time, and resources to charitable causes. Talent is given paid time off to volunteer, aligning their personal values with the company's mission.

Salesforce's compensation packages are competitive, but it's the alignment of personal and corporate values that drives retention. Talent stays not just for the salary but because they believe in the company's mission to create a positive social impact. This combination of purpose and rewards helps Salesforce attract and retain top talent committed to growing with the company.

A PERSONAL EXAMPLE: A FAMILY-OWNED BUSINESS AND LONG-TERM COMMITMENT

My father worked for 45 years in a family-run company that provided access to clean drinking water.

Despite receiving higher-paying offers from competitors, he remained loyal because:

- He was deeply connected to the company's mission.

- He felt respected and fairly compensated for his work.

Throughout his career, his contributions were recognized and aligned with the company's success. This sense of purpose and fairness kept him engaged for decades, proving that the right fit isn't just about financial rewards; it's about people who believe in your mission and feel valued.

FROM HIRING TO ONBOARDING: WHY FIRST IMPRESSIONS MATTER

Hiring the right talent is only half the battle; onboarding them effectively is just as crucial.

Even the best-fit candidates can fail if the onboarding process is weak or disorganized.

One human capital director shared, "As an HR person, if you onboard an excellent candidate, and no one takes care of them properly, it's frustrating. You know they could have thrived."

This applies even more to senior hires, who bring skills and experience but may struggle if onboarding is mismanaged.

THE HONEYMOON PHASE: SETTING THE RIGHT FOUNDATION

Onboarding should be treated as a honeymoon period, a time for new hires to build a strong connection with the company before facing inevitable challenges.

If a new hire is thrown into chaos with no proper guidance, their enthusiasm fades quickly.

A structured, supportive onboarding process builds lasting relationships and trust.

This is true not only for new talent but also for those returning after a sabbatical or maternity leave. An intentional and supportive onboarding process helps build lasting relationships between the talent and the company.

THE RISKS OF HIRING FROM LARGE CORPORATIONS

Hiring senior executives from large corporations comes with unique challenges. While they bring valuable experience, they also bring:

- Corporate cultural influences that may not align with your fast-scaling company

- A structured mindset, which may not work in an agile, high-growth environment

This doesn't mean all corporate hires will struggle, but it does mean that you must assess their adaptability to a faster, leaner, more dynamic culture.

The solution?

- Be transparent about your company culture from the hiring process.

- Ensure new hires understand the agility and pace required in a growing company.

- Structure onboarding to align senior hires with company values early.

HOW TO GET ONBOARDING RIGHT

To make onboarding effective and meaningful, here's a practical approach:

1. **Assign a Buddy and a Mentor to a new hire**

   A structured onboarding process that includes a buddy and a mentor creates an empowering and welcoming experience:

   - The buddy handles daily guidance, ensuring the new hire feels supported.

   - The mentor provides broader insights, helping the new hire connect with the company's mission and strategy.

Supporting Data:

- Companies with structured onboarding programs improve retention by 82 percent and productivity by 70 percent *(SHRM)*.

- New hires who are assigned mentors or buddies are 23 percent more likely to stay beyond their first year *(HBR)*.

2. **Create Meaningful Connections**

When a mentor or buddy voluntarily steps up to guide a new hire, it creates an immediate sense of worth and belonging.

This meaningful connection:

- Eases anxieties and builds confidence
- Signals that the new hire is valued as a person, not just a resource
- Encourages deeper engagement and faster adaptation to the company's mission

Over time, these personal relationships ripple across the organization, strengthening team culture, fostering loyalty, and ensuring long-term retention.

This means leading a company where every team member feels seen, appreciated, and united by shared values, creating a powerful foundation for scaling impact.

3. **Customize the Process**

For senior hires, cultural integration is more important than technical training.

Why This Matters:

- A leader who aligns with the company's values will amplify its vision.

- A misaligned leader can slow growth, create bottlenecks, or disrupt the culture.

Customizing the onboarding process for senior hires ensures they receive tailored support focusing on cultural integration and leadership alignment.

This allows them to:

- Adapt quickly to the company's culture

- Step confidently into their roles without friction

- Strengthen, rather than dilute, the company's mission

By aligning senior hires with your values from the start, you create a ripple effect of loyalty, momentum, and purpose-driven leadership.

THE KEY TO RETENTION: BUILDING RELATIONSHIPS

When you focus on finding the right fit and providing a strong onboarding experience, you build a team that is:

- Invested in your company's mission

- Loyal, engaged, and high-performing

- A key driver of sustainable growth

I prepared cheat sheets that summarize the step-by-step action plan to attract and retain high-performing talent, which you can download here:
www.leilalahbabi.com/impactatscalecheatsheets.

Now that you are clear on your mission, key areas of focus, and culture and have the right talent to help you scale, it's time to scale yourself.

As your company grows, so do the challenges, risks, and complexities. To ensure long-term success, you must build resilience, adaptability, and leadership strength to keep scaling without breaking.

Let's explore how to prepare yourself for sustainable growth.

STEP 3:
SCALE YOURSELF (THE CEO)

SUMMARY

Scaling yourself is the most powerful lever for your business growth. To scale your company effectively, you must first scale your leadership. That means expanding your power, refining your skills, and elevating your role to unlock new levels of impact and freedom. This chapter provides a step-by-step approach to transforming your leadership mindset, decision-making, and influence to build a thriving, high-performance organization.

Scaling your leadership is structured into three actionable strategies:

- **Expand Your Leadership Capacity:** Navigate increasing complexity with confidence by mastering emotional intelligence, strategic clarity, and resilience. By transforming challenges into opportunities, you will create a high-trust, high-performance culture where alignment and engagement drive success.

- **Lead for Innovation and Growth:** Attract top talent, foster a learning culture, and empower your team to take ownership. By shifting from directive management to leadership that inspires, you will cultivate adaptability, expertise, and sustainable business growth.

- **Shift from Operations to Visionary Leadership:** Move beyond daily execution to focus on long-term strategy, enabling your team to lead with accountability. By balancing care with tough decisions, you will build a scalable, resilient organization rooted in shared values.

Together, these three strategies provide a clear, actionable framework for scaling yourself as a leader. By implementing them, you will ensure that your leadership fuels alignment, accountability, and long-term success, allowing both you and your company to thrive.

Let's dive into how to implement each.

Scale your Personal Power

The success or failure of a company starts with its founder. Your ability to lead, scale, and embody your vision directly shapes your company's trajectory. Just as strong leadership can propel a company forward, uncontrolled emotions, poor decision-making, and lack of resilience can just as easily cause its downfall.

Scaling a company starts with scaling yourself. If you fail to develop the emotional resilience, clarity, and leadership presence your business requires, your company will struggle to scale sustainably.

The Growth Curve of Emotional Resilience

I once attended an immersion for personal and professional growth, where a seasoned entrepreneur shared a picture that stayed with me: "The more you grow, the less intensely you experience your emotions."

Think about your first client or your first big payment. How did it feel when that initial success landed? Now, if a similar client were to join your business today, would the emotional impact be as intense? Probably not.

The same applies to setbacks. Remember your first customer complaint or the first time someone criticized your work? Maybe it was a bad online review or, worse, a business conflict involving someone close to you. The emotions you felt then were likely overwhelming.

Now, think about how you would handle those same situations today. If your response is, "I'd manage it better now," that's proof of growth. However, if the emotional impact would still be just as intense, you've identified a leverage point for personal growth. Strengthening your ability to regulate emotions in high-stakes situations will directly impact your ability to scale your company effectively.

Many founders experience this shift in how they perceive success and setbacks. Early in your business, making $5,000 felt exhilarating. Now, the excitement of making even $100,000 might have dulled. While it's natural for achievements to normalize, the goal isn't to neutralize your emotions. Instead, it's to continue experiencing joy and gratitude in each milestone while building the resilience needed to handle increasing complexity.

This is the core of scaling your personal power.

LEADERS WHO LET EMOTIONS TAKE OVER—AND PAID THE PRICE

- Travis Kalanick (Uber) built a groundbreaking company, but his inability to regulate his emotions in high-pressure situations—including public outbursts and conflicts—led to his downfall. The toxic culture at Uber, largely shaped by his behavior, resulted in his forced resignation.

- Amy Winehouse, an incredibly talented singer, struggled with fame and emotional instability, leading to self-destruction despite massive success. Without emotional resilience, external success does not guarantee sustainability.

LEADERS WHO BUILT RESILIENCE – AND THRIVED

- Yvon Chouinard (Patagonia) scaled Patagonia by leading with emotional intelligence, purpose, and humility. He actively stepped back, built a leadership team that aligned with his values, and created a company culture that thrived without micromanagement or ego-driven leadership. His ability to stay grounded despite Patagonia's massive success allowed the company to maintain its mission while scaling globally.

- Oprah Winfrey faced immense public scrutiny and business challenges yet consistently grounded herself in self-awareness, resilience, and purpose-driven leadership. She leveraged emotional intelligence to navigate challenges, turning setbacks into opportunities for reinvention and growth.

Scaling your company hinges on your ability to manage emotions under pressure. Often, leaders who struggle with emotional resilience struggle with scaling sustainably.

The difference? Emotionally resilient leaders use challenges as leverage for growth. Those who fail to manage emotions risk self-sabotage and business failure.

SCALING YOUR PERSONAL POWER: A STRATEGIC NECESSITY

To scale, you need to equip yourself to handle setbacks, uncertainty, and high-stakes decisions, all while maintaining your energy, clarity, and well-being.

Many founders struggle to disconnect from work. Even on vacation, they find themselves checking Slack, responding to emails, and feeling responsible for every issue. One founder I interviewed shared: "Even when I step away physically, my mind is still at work. I can't disconnect because I feel responsible for both the business and my team."

This constant engagement drains mental energy and leads to burnout, poor decision-making, and emotional fatigue that hinder business growth.

Scaling yourself is gaining more leverage rather than working harder.

The good news is it's a learnable skill.

A Simple Framework for Emotional Growth

There are countless leadership frameworks and emotional intelligence assessments, but complexity isn't the goal. Instead of chasing the perfect framework, start where you are and focus on the most pressing emotional challenges you face today.

1. **Identify Your Growth Areas**: What are the emotional triggers that disrupt your decision-making or leadership effectiveness? Reflect on past experiences and identify patterns.

2. **Choose an Approach That Works for You**: Whether it's coaching, mindfulness, leadership training, or therapy, the method matters less than the progress. The best approach is the one that helps you build resilience and clarity.

3. **Measure Progress by Actions, Not Tests**: Don't rely on assessments or external validation. The real test of emotional growth is whether you can handle challenges with more clarity, calmness, and precision than before.

If you're making better decisions, responding to setbacks with composure, and leading with confidence, you're scaling your personal power effectively.

WHY THIS MATTERS

Emotional intelligence doesn't just impact you; it shapes your entire organization.

You've likely heard the phrase, "People don't quit bad jobs; they quit bad bosses."

This is especially true for high-performing talent. Talented individuals seek leaders who are self-aware, emotionally intelligent, and capable of creating an environment of trust and growth.

Companies with low emotional intelligence experience:

- High turnover due to poor leadership

- Low engagement from talent who feel undervalued

- Toxic work cultures that slow down innovation and scaling

In contrast, companies that prioritize emotional intelligence see:

- Higher retention rates from engaged, purpose-driven talent

- Stronger collaboration and innovation driven by trust

- Smoother scaling with less internal friction

Scaling a Business = Scaling Emotional Intelligence

Your company will only grow as far as you do.

Scaling your personal power as a founder makes you a better leader and creates an environment where your team thrives, your company scales with less resistance, and your mission expands with clarity, stability, and impact.

Scaling yourself is a prerequisite for sustainable business success.

Final Thought: The Ripple Effect of Emotional Leadership

Your emotional intelligence sets the tone for your company's culture, performance, and long-term success.

By strengthening your resilience, decision-making, and leadership presence, you don't just become a better leader; you build a company that scales with integrity, impact, and stability.

Let's move forward into the next chapter, where we'll explore how to sustain high performance while maintaining balance as a leader.

Scale your Skills

What if the biggest bottleneck in your company's growth wasn't your market, your competition, or even your team, but you? Many CEOs assume that once they've set a vision, execution is someone else's job. However, in reality, when leaders don't evolve, companies stagnate. A lack of knowledge in key areas leads to blind spots, costly mistakes, and missed opportunities. To scale your company, you must first scale yourself and your skills.

The Cost of Not Scaling Your Skills

Companies that fail to scale often suffer from a lack of leadership depth. Here's what happens when CEOs fail to develop their understanding of key business areas:

- **Blockbuster's Leadership Failure:** While Netflix's Reed Hastings immersed himself in digital streaming trends, Blockbuster's leadership remained disconnected from consumer behavior shifts. This failure to understand digital transformation led to their downfall.

- **Kodak's Missed Opportunity:** Kodak's leaders invented the first digital camera but failed to invest in it because they didn't understand how digital technology would reshape the industry. A lack of foresight and technical literacy cost them their market dominance.

- **BlackBerry's Decline:** As Apple and Google innovated rapidly, BlackBerry's leadership failed to recognize the importance of app ecosystems and touchscreen technology. Their inability to adapt led to their collapse.

To scale your company, you must first scale yourself. If you don't have a foundational understanding of each area of your business—whether marketing, sales, finance, or operations—you won't be able to guide your team effectively. This doesn't mean becoming an expert in every area, but investing at least 20 hours in learning the basics ensures you can challenge, support, and lead effectively.

If you don't understand how something works, you won't be able to delegate it properly. Leaders who fail to scale their skills often make costly mistakes because they can't spot inefficiencies or ask the right questions. Kodak exemplifies this. While they invented the first digital camera, leadership failed to capitalize on the technology due to a lack of understanding, leading to their decline.

BACK TO BASICS

To scale effectively, invest time in learning the fundamentals of every core function of your business. This knowledge empowers you to hire the right people, ask the right questions, and ensure your team stays on track.

1. Invest in Learning the Basics

You are not required to master every skill in the company, but you should know enough to manage those who do. If marketing is critical to your company's growth, invest time in learning the fundamentals of digital marketing—how campaigns are structured, what metrics matter, and how success is measured. The same applies to finance, operations, and people management.

Example: Brian Chesky (Airbnb) Brian Chesky didn't just delegate key business functions; he immersed himself in marketing, finance, operations, and customer psychology.

This hands-on approach had a significant financial impact, especially during the COVID-19 pandemic. In early 2020, Airbnb faced an 80 percent drop in revenue over eight weeks, forcing difficult decisions, including layoffs.

Chesky personally took charge of marketing efforts, eliminating nearly a billion dollars in marketing costs and focusing on direct communication and press engagements. This hands-on strategy preserved cash while maintaining the company's public presence. As a result, Airbnb transitioned from losing hundreds of millions to generating $3.4 billion in free cash flow by 2022, with nearly 40 percent of its revenue converting to free cash flow.

2. Become a Teacher and Storyteller

As your company scales, your role will increasingly involve transferring your vision and knowledge to others. Great leaders are also great storytellers. They can take complex ideas and distill them into something that inspires and engages their team. Learning how to teach and tell stories will make you a more effective CEO and strengthen leadership across your organization.

Example: Howard Schultz (Starbucks)

Howard Schultz rescued Starbucks from a 42 percent stock drop in 2007 by leveraging storytelling to redefine its mission as a "third place" between home and work, reigniting customer loyalty and financial growth. His commitment to employee well-being, including healthcare for part-timers and stock ownership programs, helped Starbucks scale into an over $100 billion brand, proving that visionary leadership and narrative-driven culture drive long-term success.

3. Hire People Better Than You and Learn From Them

Once you understand the basics, hire experts in their fields but don't stop there. Learn from them. Let them teach you the advanced aspects of their domain. This will deepen your knowledge, strengthen relationships, and build a culture of mutual growth.

Example: Satya Nadella (Microsoft)
When Satya Nadella took over Microsoft, he emphasized a growth mindset throughout the organization. He hired top talent, learned from them, and fostered a culture of learning and collaboration. This allowed Microsoft to innovate rapidly and transform into a leader in cloud computing. The company's market capitalization grew from around $300 billion in 2014 to over $2 trillion by 2021, showcasing the impact of leadership that values learning and adaptation.

4. Encourage a Learning Culture

Leaders who scale effectively don't just focus on their growth; they create a culture where learning is valued across the company. When your team sees that you're continuously learning, they're more likely to follow suit. Encourage team members to teach each other and share new insights. This fosters continuous development, strengthens relationships, and helps the entire company scale.

Example: Salesforce
Salesforce scaled into an over $250 billion company with over 20 percent CRM market share by fostering a learning culture through its Trailhead platform, which has upskilled over 4 million users, boosting internal mobility and retention. Under Marc Benioff's leadership, this commitment to continuous learning fueled revenue growth from $5 billion

in 2015 to $34 billion in 2023, proving that a values-driven, knowledge-sharing culture accelerates both financial success and employee engagement.

WHAT IF YOU DON'T SCALE YOUR SKILLS?

If you don't invest in scaling your skills, you risk losing control over your company's direction. A CEO who can't challenge or guide their team leaves decision-making to others, leading to misalignment with company goals. This can result in costly mistakes because of a lack of critical oversight.

Consider BlackBerry's decline. Its leadership failed to evolve with the smartphone market, while Apple and Google rapidly innovated. Similarly, WeWork's Adam Neumann lacked the leadership skills to transition from visionary founder to operational leader, costing the company billions. These failures highlight what happens when CEOs don't invest in their own growth.

As a founder, you are the heartbeat of your organization. To grow a business that reflects your vision, you must first grow your capacity to lead, guide, and inspire. Invest in understanding the fundamentals of each business function so you can guide and support your team effectively.

This isn't about micromanaging but about equipping yourself with enough understanding to ask the right questions, challenge assumptions, and provide meaningful direction. A well-rounded leader fosters trust, enabling teams to work with greater focus, clarity, and autonomy.

Challenge: Identify one business area you need to strengthen. Commit to investing 20 hours in learning the basics. When leaders grow, businesses thrive.

The next and last challenge before moving to your team is to scale your role. This is what we will tackle in the next chapter.

Scale your Role

As your company grows, so must your role as a leader. Scaling a company isn't just about expanding operations or driving more revenue. It's about evolving from being deeply involved in the details to becoming the strategist and people manager your business needs to thrive. This transition is crucial because the skills that got you here won't necessarily take you to the next stage of growth. If you stay stuck in the role of the doer, you'll prevent your company from scaling beyond your bandwidth and capabilities.

Scaling involves multiple stages, much like the spiral metaphor used in the mission chapter. You may find yourself delegating responsibilities you once managed, only to face another round of delegation at a higher level. You are not in the same place again but rather facing a similar challenge a few levels up.

The Two Common Traps Leaders Face

In my experience as a strategy consultant, I've seen leaders fall into two common traps when trying to scale their roles.

1. **Over-Reliance on HR and a Profit-Only Focus**
   o Some leaders view people management as an administrative task, heavily relying on HR while focusing solely on profit. While this may free up time, it can disconnect you from the human side of your business, leading to disengagement, poor performance, and high turnover.

○ Over time, this detachment can result in burnout and regret as the business evolves into a profit-driven machine misaligned with your values and original vision.

2. **Over-Prioritizing People Without Accountability**

○ Other leaders focus primarily on the human aspects of the business and avoid tough decisions for fear of harming relationships. This may foster initial harmony but creates inefficiencies, frustrates high-performing team members, and erodes accountability.

○ As talent leaves and culture deteriorates, leaders feel trapped between protecting relationships and safeguarding the business. This avoidance can ultimately derail your company's ability to scale.

Both approaches can have drastic consequences on your business, culture, and personal well-being.

Shift from Control to Accountability

One of the biggest mistakes I've seen leaders make is staying overly involved in day-to-day details, micromanaging their team, and controlling every outcome. This leads to a lack of empowerment, where your talent depends on you for every decision, keeping you stuck in a cycle of constant problem-solving.

Buurtzorg, a Dutch home healthcare organization, eliminated hierarchical management structures and empowered nurses to self-organize. Teams make their own staffing decisions, manage schedules, and ensure patient care without direct oversight from managers.

Buurtzorg Nederland has experienced significant growth over the years. By 2014, the organization reported an annual turnover of €280 million. As of 2023, estimates suggest that Buurtzorg's annual revenue has reached approximately $5 billion.

This substantial increase reflects Buurtzorg's expansion and the widespread adoption of its innovative, nurse-led self-management model in home healthcare.

MOVE FROM TECHNICIAN TO STRATEGIST

In the early days, being involved in every part of the business is necessary. Whether it's marketing, sales, product development, or customer service, you've likely had hands-on experience. However, as the company scales, remaining the doer in every aspect becomes unsustainable.

Leaders who fail to transition from technician to strategist end up creating a job for themselves rather than building a scalable business.

Example: Sara Blakely (Spanx)
When she founded Spanx, Sara Blakely was heavily involved in every detail: designing products, selling door-to-door, and even handling legal matters herself. As Spanx grew, she transitioned from being the primary creator to focusing on brand vision and strategic partnerships, allowing a team of experts to manage operations. Her shift enabled Spanx to scale into a billion-dollar company without being bottlenecked by her involvement in daily operations.

Balancing People and Profit: The Fine Line

Scaling your role requires balancing care for your people with the critical decisions needed to sustain the business. Leaders who prioritize profits over people risk creating a disengaged workforce. Conversely, leaders who hesitate to make difficult choices to protect relationships often allow inefficiencies to linger, harming long-term success.

Example: Satya Nadella (Microsoft)
Nadella successfully balanced people and performance by restructuring teams, letting go of individuals misaligned with Microsoft's evolving mission, and reinforcing a culture of growth and innovation. His leadership revitalized the company, growing its market capitalization from $300 billion in 2014 to over $2 trillion by 2021.

People Strategy as a Core Skill

People management is not just an HR task; it's a strategic function that determines your company's long-term success. Treating it as an afterthought limits your ability to scale.

Example: Bob Chapman (Barry-Wehmiller)
Bob Chapman revolutionized the manufacturing industry by embedding Truly Human Leadership, prioritizing employee well-being, emotional intelligence, and leadership development, turning Barry-Wehmiller into a "people-first" powerhouse. This human-centered approach scaled revenue from $20 million to over $3 billion, proving that investing in people drives both business success and lasting impact.

Let Them Go with Fairness

When someone isn't the right fit for your company, the best course of action is to let them go fairly and respectfully. Keeping underperforming employees signals to your team that performance and culture are not priorities, which can weaken morale and make your high-performing talent question themselves.

Fair offboarding means providing severance and career support and treating people with dignity. Doing so not only preserves morale but also reinforces a culture of performance and integrity.

Scaling Your Role to Scale Your Company

When you evolve from being the technician and doer to the strategist and people manager, you shift from control to accountability. This transition empowers your team to take ownership, fosters autonomy, and ensures alignment between your company's values and operational growth.

By scaling your role effectively, you create space for your company to grow sustainably, balancing financial performance with a thriving company culture.

I've prepared cheat sheets summarizing the step-by-step action plan to scale yourself as a CEO. Download them here for reference: **leilalahbabi.com/impactatscalecheatsheets**

Once you've done that, it's time to scale this transformation across your organization. That's what we'll explore in the next step.

STEP 4:
SCALE YOUR TEAM
PERFORMANCE

SUMMARY

Empowering your team is essential to scaling your business. By elevating their abilities, redefining their roles, and fostering a culture of trust and accountability, you will create a resilient, high-performing workforce that drives sustainable growth. This chapter provides a step-by-step approach to unlocking your team's full potential while ensuring alignment with your company's mission.

Scaling your team is structured into three actionable strategies:

- **Foster Ownership and Engagement:** Build an environment where talent feels trusted, valued, and motivated to take the initiative. By cultivating a culture of collaboration and innovation, you will create a resilient workforce that thrives on accountability and shared success.

- **Develop Confidence and Performance:** Ensure your team can perform effectively in their roles by fostering continuous learning and improvement. By enhancing individual productivity and team synergy, you will elevate both employee satisfaction and overall organizational success.

- **Align Strengths with Strategic Impact:** Enable your team to focus on their highest-value contributions, ensuring seamless execution—even in remote environments. By prioritizing autonomy and efficiency, you will build a well-aligned organization poised for sustainable, scalable success.

Together, these three strategies provide a clear, actionable framework for scaling your team with intention. By implementing them, you will cultivate a workforce that not only delivers results but also amplifies your company's mission with passion and purpose.

Let's dive into how to implement each.

SCALE THE POWER OF YOUR TEAM (BREAKING FREE FROM LIMITING PATTERNS)

In a well-known experiment, monkeys were placed in a cage with bananas hanging from the ceiling. Every time a monkey tried to grab the bananas, it was sprayed with cold water, teaching it not to try again. Even after all the original monkeys were replaced with new ones, the behavior persisted. None of the new monkeys had experienced the cold water, yet they still stopped each other from reaching the bananas simply following what they had observed.

Some leaders take this story to mean they should start fresh by replacing all staff to change a culture. However, I see it differently. We are not monkeys. Unlike animals bound by instinct, humans have the ability to reflect, question ingrained patterns, and choose new paths. With the right leadership, care, and opportunities for growth, people can unlearn outdated behaviors and adopt new, aligned ones. The goal isn't to replace your team but to empower them to break free from inherited limitations.

WE ARE BORN TO LEARN

Humans are wired for growth. Unlike animals that rely on fixed instincts, we possess the ability to evolve, consciously challenging old patterns, reflecting on behaviors, and choosing intentional change. Growth, both personal and professional, is an essential part of this journey, laying the foundation for building resilient teams and organizations. As leaders, we must harness this natural ability not just for ourselves but for our teams.

Your Team Is an Extension of Who You Are

The most successful companies embody the personality and values of their founders. For example, Stripe's precision and focus on excellence reflect Patrick Collison's Approach, while Airbnb's openness and creativity mirror Brian Chesky's mindset. These companies succeed by being true to their founders' vision, not by copying others.

Early Google felt like a university, driven by Larry Page and Sergey Brin's academic mindset. Meanwhile, Facebook reflected Mark Zuckerberg's fast-paced, scrappy culture. These unique identities were critical to their growth. Copying another company's practices won't work; success comes from building authentically and staying aligned with your strengths and values.

As your company grows, so does the pressure on you, the founder, to maintain the vision and culture that initially set the company apart. It's not uncommon to see your role evolve from "doing everything" to focusing on higher-level strategy. Just as you scale your business and yourself, it's also important to scale your team by cascading the leadership through your organization. By doing so, you ensure your company's growth is sustainable for the business, for your team, and for yourself as an individual.

Cascading and Embedded Leadership

Leadership is not about authority or hierarchy; it's a mindset. It's the ability to influence, inspire, and cultivate excellence at every level of the organization. This requires cascading leadership; leadership behaviors must flow from you, the founder, to executives and throughout the workforce.

Too often, companies focus leadership development on top executives while neglecting the broader workforce. However, true impact occurs when everyone in the organization feels empowered to lead. Talent thrives when they are trusted to take initiative and make decisions that align with the company's mission.

A compelling example of cascading leadership comes from Dr. Emile Jeuken's research. His study of 1,656 Dutch military peacekeepers showed that trust in leadership cascades across multiple hierarchical levels, positively impacting talent engagement and performance. This finding underscores that when leadership is modeled and embodied at the top, it ripples through the ranks, improving morale and productivity throughout the organization.

AUTHENTICITY OVER FRAMEWORKS

Embodied leadership, leading by example, lies at the heart of cascading leadership. When you truly live your values, people naturally follow. While some individuals lead intuitively, others prefer to be guided to develop their leadership skills. Frameworks can help clarify what good leadership looks like, but they are just a starting point.

I often tell clients, "Leadership isn't about frameworks; it's about authenticity." Frameworks speak to the mind, but great leadership speaks to the heart. It's an emotional connection between people that builds trust and engagement. You can't fake or force it; it must be embodied so it can cascade through your organization.

Rather than relying heavily on frameworks, I focus on authentic sharing. When working with clients, I ask:

- Who are the great leaders you know?

- Why are you doing what you do?

- What wakes you up at night?

By sitting down with these leaders, we uncover not just their thoughts but their emotions and body sensations about leadership. This process, inspired by mindfulness, creates a leadership blueprint that resonates with the company's unique culture, condensing years of experience into teachable moments that accelerate learning.

TAKING CARE OF YOUR PEOPLE SO THEY CAN TAKE CARE OF YOUR BUSINESS

We bring our whole selves to work and home. Our emotions, challenges, and aspirations don't switch off when we walk through the office door. Leaders who recognize this create healthier, more sustainable work environments. Personal challenges that go unaddressed can quietly erode performance and morale, leading to burnout and disengagement.

Creating a culture of care starts with leaders showing vulnerability and authenticity. Leaders who allow themselves to be human—expressing emotions thoughtfully and making decisions from a grounded place—build trust and foster loyalty. This sets the tone for talent to do the same, creating a work environment where authenticity and mutual support thrive.

Companies like Salesforce and Southwest Airlines demonstrate how care drives performance. Salesforce offers mental health programs and flexible work policies, enabling talent to balance personal and professional challenges. Southwest's "People First" philosophy has fostered loyalty, resulting in one of the lowest turnover rates in the airline industry. These companies show that genuine care leads to higher engagement, retention, and profitability.

Just as leadership cascades through every level, care flows throughout the organization. When you take care of your people, your people, in turn, take care of your business.

PROVIDING OPPORTUNITIES FOR PERSONAL GROWTH

Talent performs at their best when they operate from their "higher self," a state of presence, creativity, and intentional action. The "higher self" means stepping out of reactive fight-or-flight mode and approaching challenges with clarity and courage. It's about breaking old norms—like the monkeys in the cage—and creating new ways of working based on intentional decisions, not fear.

Emotional and financial security are important for talent to access their higher self. Without security, people remain in survival mode, limiting their ability to innovate or collaborate. You can help by providing mental health support, wellness programs, and coaching, enabling talent to stay grounded and perform their best.

Operating from the higher self was one of the most transformative shifts in my personal journey. When I moved from fear-driven actions to intentional leadership, I unlocked new skills, embraced a growth mindset, and achieved far more than I thought possible. The impact of this shift was profound—not only on my career but also on my personal well-being.

For instance, a talent operating from their higher self might approach a project setback with curiosity and collaboration rather than frustration and blame. This kind of intentional leadership sets the stage for creativity and innovation.

Imagine an organization where every talent operates from their higher self. Creativity, collaboration, and engagement would flourish. Talent would make thoughtful, courageous decisions and contribute meaningfully to the company's mission. The ripple effects of such a culture would extend far beyond individual performance, transforming the company as a whole.

Scale Your Team's Skills With Precision

A recurring fear among leaders is investing in their people only to see them leave. In interviews, I often heard concerns like, "What if we train them, and they leave?" or, "They'll take our know-how into a competitive market."

This fear is understandable, especially in industries like fintech, where replacing top performers is tough, and the investment in onboarding and training can feel like a gamble. However, the real question is not whether they might leave; it's what happens if they stay without the right skills.

Neglecting talent development can leave you with disengaged or underperforming talent. These individuals, whether they remain with your organization or move on, can negatively impact your reputation.

On the other hand, investing in their growth is a win-win strategy. If they stay, they elevate your organization's performance; if they leave, they become brand ambassadors, carrying your company's values into future roles. Just like alumni networks at universities, former talent can become valuable partners, clients, or advocates, creating long-term benefits for your organization.

A compelling example of the power of investing in people comes from a construction company an interviewed change-maker told me about. Within 18 months of transforming a company's internal culture, it became known for treating people differently, which started attracting talent from competitors.

Clients noticed the shift, asking, "What are you doing differently?" This illustrates how building a magnetic culture through targeted development not only retains talent but also draws top performers from the outside.

Scaling a company is impossible without scaling the skills and relationships of your team. When you focus on growing people, you're building a workforce that contributes meaningfully during their tenure and extends your organization's reach long after. This ripple effect strengthens your brand, attracts new talent, and opens the door to future opportunities.

The Key: Focus on Quality Over Quantity

Effective learning and development is about giving the talent the skills that will help them better deliver their work. Think again about the boat vs. the surfing metaphor. Success isn't about going through a heavy library of courses; it's about mastering the essentials that help you ride the right wave at the right moment.

Too often, companies offer a buffet of e-learning options, assuming more is better. However, this approach leads to what I call "infobesity"—an overload of information without practical value.

The key is to focus on *quality*, not *quantity*. Instead of overwhelming talent with irrelevant content, give them targeted, relevant training that aligns with their roles and goals. This not only improves individual performance but also provides a better return on investment (ROI) for your L&D efforts. Often, cutting costs by reducing L&D spending backfires; true savings come from investing strategically in what matters most.

To scale your team's skills with precision, follow these guiding principles:

1. **Identify Key Skills:**

   o Prioritize the specific skills that will help your team members excel in their current roles and evolve into future leaders, ensuring their growth aligns with your business's strategic goals.

   o By focusing on relevant skills, you'll empower talent to contribute meaningfully and drive measurable progress, building their confidence as they see their efforts translate into success.

2. **Deliver Targeted, High-Impact Learning:**

   o Instead of drowning talent in a sea of courses, provide concise, well-designed training that solves real challenges.

   o When learning is aligned with daily tasks, talent can immediately apply what they've learned.

3. **Integrate Learning into Daily Work:**

   o Training is most effective when it's embedded into everyday work.

o Use hands-on coaching, real-time feedback, and collaborative problem-solving to ensure knowledge sticks.

4. **Measure Outcomes, Not Participation:**

o The success of learning and development efforts lies in the application of learning, not the number of courses completed.

o Shift your focus from attendance metrics to performance improvements and real-world outcomes.

RIDING THE WAVE TOGETHER

Imagine if every talent in your organization had the skills required to excel right on time. Picture a workplace where talent isn't burdened by irrelevant information but is equipped to navigate their roles confidently. They know what to do, how to do it, and why it matters—making them more effective, engaged, and aligned with the company's mission.

With this focused approach, your team will thrive in their roles and elevate the entire organization's performance. Talent will feel empowered and motivated to contribute their best work, and the company will benefit from stronger collaboration, innovation, and sustained growth.

When investments yield tangible results, you can let go of slashing learning and development budgets. Like surfing, it is about doing the right things at the right time. By focusing on quality, relevance, and real-world application, you unlock the full potential of your team, creating a culture that can adapt, innovate, and thrive in a constantly evolving landscape.

Scale Roles and Change The Game

Scaling a team is about changing the game. Think of it like moving from basketball to football. In a small, agile team, everyone plays multiple roles, just like basketball players who switch between offense and defense. When your team starts playing with the football mindset as your business grows, each team player will focus on a specific position, contributing to the team's strategy in a defined way.

When you narrow the focus for each team member, they master their role instead of taking on more general tasks. This sense of excellence in one thing creates a collective force that drives impact. It's the difference between trying to catch every wave versus picking the right one to surf. A clear, focused role ensures talent isn't stretched too thin but is positioned to deliver meaningful results.

Rethinking Support Functions: From Cost Centers to Value Creators

"Money is in the back end," said one of my favorite mentors, and he is right.

Traditionally, companies have separated revenue-generating roles from support functions like finance, operations, or IT. These support functions are often viewed as cost centers, with fixed salaries, limited rewards, and minimal recognition. This mindset underestimates their value, leading to underappreciation, high turnover, and operational inefficiencies.

In reality, support teams are the backbone of an organization. Imagine a household without anyone managing day-to-day tasks like cooking or childcare—productivity would collapse.

Similarly, if support functions aren't efficient, front-line teams can't perform at their best.

Rather than treating support roles as invisible or replaceable, companies need to shift their perspective. Support functions should be recognized as strategic partners contributing to the company's overall success. To do this:

1. **Transform Support Functions into Strategic Value Drivers:**

   o Elevate your support teams from being perceived as cost centers to becoming essential engines of efficiency, innovation, and growth.

   o As your company scales and operations grow more complex, their contributions become pivotal for sustainable performance.

   o Empowering these teams to take ownership fosters a culture of collaboration where every individual feels they're a vital part of your mission.

   o Imagine the relief and pride of seeing your company operate as a unified force, with every department aligned to drive impact, amplify your vision, and build a legacy that stands the test of time.

2. **Celebrate the Invisible Champions:**

   o Performance metrics can extend beyond sales to include the invaluable contributions of support roles.

   o By defining clear performance goals tied to fair compensation and heartfelt recognition, you acknowledge the essential work these teams do to keep your mission alive.

○ This validation builds loyalty and ignites a culture of continuous improvement where everyone feels motivated to excel.

○ As your support teams feel truly seen and valued, their commitment deepens, creating a ripple effect of positivity and alignment throughout the organization.

○ Ultimately, by honoring meaningful contributions, you're fostering a sense of shared purpose.

○ This alignment propels your mission forward with unstoppable momentum, fueling both your business growth and your vision for a better world.

Managing Multicultural Teams and Remote Work

The rise of remote work has opened access to global talent, enabling companies to build multicultural teams. However, managing a distributed workforce requires new approaches to trust, accountability, and connection.

With remote teams, when you provide clear expectations, set measurable goals, and shift from a time-based to a results-oriented evaluation model, you ensure accountability and create a path to success. As one interviewed leader explained, "We don't control how people spend their time, but we make sure they're accountable for their output."

Intentional connection is also crucial. Remote teams thrive when they have opportunities to build personal relationships. Companies that succeed in this space invest in face-to-face gatherings, such as annual retreats or project-based meetups.

These events help talent bond, fostering a sense of belonging that's difficult to achieve through virtual meetings alone.

Additionally, when remote teams embrace cultural sensitivity and cross-cultural communication, working across borders brings diverse perspectives. When you provide the tools to navigate cultural differences effectively and training programs that promote cultural awareness, you enhance collaboration and prevent misunderstandings, ensuring smoother teamwork.

LEVERAGING AI: ENHANCING, NOT REPLACING, HUMAN TALENT

AI is about amplifying people's capabilities, not replacing them. It takes over repetitive tasks, freeing talent to focus on creative, strategic, and high-impact work. When implemented effectively, AI enables faster decision-making, more efficient operations, and improved innovation.

AI offers particular value when integrated into workflows that require data processing. For example, it can automate data collection, process surveys, and summarize key meeting points, allowing your team to focus on analysis and problem-solving rather than administrative work.

However, AI is only as good as the strategy behind it. If your business processes are flawed, AI will amplify those flaws. However, with a clear vision and aligned goals, AI can become a powerful tool for scaling operations. It accelerates what's working, helping you reach your objectives faster without compromising quality or human connection.

The key to leveraging AI is intentionality. AI is a tool, not a solution. It works best when it enhances processes that are already aligned with your company's values and objectives.

The goal is to use AI to remove friction, freeing talent to innovate, collaborate, and drive sustainable growth.

A FUTURE OF EMPOWERED TEAMS AND SEAMLESS GROWTH

Imagine a company where every team member knows their role with precision—like a football player on the field, fully aware of their position and responsibilities. Picture a workplace where support functions are seen as integral value drivers, not invisible cost centers. Envision a remote, multicultural workforce connected by shared goals, trust, and purpose, working seamlessly across time zones.

With AI handling routine tasks and surfacing key insights, your team can focus on what truly matters: creating value, driving innovation, and building lasting relationships. Talent feels empowered, knowing that their contributions are recognized and their growth is supported.

Scaling your high-performing team members' roles is about doing the right things. By focusing on precision, valuing every role, fostering connection, and leveraging AI with purpose, your business can grow sustainably and thrive in an ever-changing world. This future is within reach, and it begins with redefining how you scale your team today.

I prepared cheat sheets that summarize the step-by-step action plan to scale your high-performing team that you can download here for reference: leilalahbabi.com/impactatscalecheatsheets

Now, you have all the ingredients to build a resilient company, but as things don't always go as planned, it's important to scale your company's adaptability to make sure it survives through the storms.

STEP 5:
SCALE YOUR ADAPTABILITY

SUMMARY

Once you've created a shared mission, attracted and developed the right talent, and built essential skills across your organization, the next step is to scale how high-performing teams collaborate and adapt to an evolving market. Developing resilience and adaptability within your company is crucial for scaling sustainably and thriving in a constantly changing environment. This chapter provides a step-by-step approach to strengthening your organization's collective intelligence, fostering continuous improvement, and preparing for long-term success.

Scaling adaptability is structured into three actionable strategies:

- **Unlock Collective Intelligence:** Build a resilient organization by empowering teams to proactively tackle challenges, solve complex problems, and drive sustainable growth. By fostering collaboration and shared ownership, you will create a company that thrives in uncertainty.

- **Embed Reflection and Iteration:** Ensure that growth is repeatable and scalable without burning out your team. By creating systems for continuous learning and adaptation, you will enable your business to evolve in alignment with both internal and external shifts.

- **Prepare for Long-Term Independence:** Step back strategically, attract investors, or plan for succession without disrupting operations. By structuring your business for sustainability, you will build an organization that remains mission-driven, highly attractive to investors, and capable of scaling its impact and legacy beyond your tenure.

Together, these three strategies provide a clear, actionable framework for scaling your organization with resilience and adaptability. By implementing them, you will future-proof your business while empowering your team to excel, ensuring that your company continues to thrive long after you step away.

Let's dive into how to implement each.

Scale the Collective Intelligence

It is funny and on purpose that this chapter comes just after the chapter that advises you to assign specific roles. Let me tell you a story to make the link between specific roles and collective intelligence.

I was hanging out with a friend of mine in the kid's playground, and I asked her about her work at a well-known financial services company. She was able to explain her daily tasks in a clear manner. She makes sure that the customer experience in the client interface is seamless.

I was then curious. "Amazing! Tell me more about the product and value proposition?" She confessed that she knows almost nothing about trading in financial markets (the industry of her company). Then, it struck me that her company was sitting on a huge opportunity of innovation: collective intelligence.

What I mean by collective intelligence is having your team collaborate to find solutions to solve the business problems your company faces. It is knowing that whatever problem your company faces, your team has your back. It's knowing that whenever any member of your team is down, the rest of the team works together to take the lead.

Collective intelligence means knowing that you don't have to constantly figure out how the market is and how to adapt to it. Instead, it's having your team come up with innovative ideas to best serve your clients and stay ahead of your competition.

How can you do that when each member of your team is solely focused on his "task"? How can you sustainably motivate people to come to work if they don't share a common purpose?

145

You can't, and when I look at my friend, she doesn't seem to care anymore about the company than just doing her job with minimal effort in the minimum time to get back to her life.

Most organizations strive for collective intelligence, but they fall short.

They drive performance management by focusing on hiring the best resumes, creating rigid plans, and streamlining individual objectives. At first glance, this strategy seems sound: Recruit top talent, structure everything, and measure success individually.

However, this doesn't work. Instead, there are consequences:

- Top talent operates in silos, focusing only on personal performance.
- The organization becomes rigid, driven solely by plans rather than adaptability.
- Talent competes for individual goals, leading to friction and misaligned efforts.

As a result:

- Toxic high performers undermine team cohesion, like a rower out of sync with the crew, disrupting the boat's rhythm.
- The organization becomes closed to innovation, locked into rigid structures and plans.
- Individual goals take priority over collective success, preventing talent from working together effectively.

Instead, a better approach is to focus on collective performance and mutual growth.

Here are two metaphors that can help.

Rowing Together: Synchronization and Leadership

In a rowing team, every rower must paddle in rhythm under clear leadership. When individual rowers pull in different directions, the team's progress stalls. Even a talented rower who refuses to sync with the group disrupts the flow, slowing everyone down.

Similarly, individual success that isn't aligned with team goals becomes a liability. Effective teams require synchronized efforts guided by clearly understood objectives and strong leadership.

Jazz Band: Innovation Through Adaptability and Collaboration

In a jazz band, musicians improvise while listening to one another, responding in real-time to create harmony. Leadership shifts fluidly, and mistakes become part of the process, fueling creativity.

Like a jazz band, companies must balance structure and improvisation to perform at their best. Teams need the freedom to experiment and innovate, which only happens when their individual tasks are in sync with the common objective and psychological safety is present, allowing talent to take risks without fear of failure or judgment.

The Positive Impact of Collective Intelligence at Scale

When collective intelligence is fully operationalized, it leads to:

- **Greater Synergy:**

    o Teams will achieve more together, which means that your company can increase its ability to cross-sell and flow from sales to operations.

    o This leads to higher sales and satisfaction levels per customer and lower selling costs because you don't need to spend any additional money on marketing to repeat business.

    o The clients already know and trust you and your team, which in the end will lead to higher revenues and higher profit by having more margin per sale with lower costs. (Selling to your current customer costs less than selling to new customers.)

- **Seamless Operations and Innovation:**

    o Collaboration and trust foster smooth operations and continuous innovation.

    o With continuous innovation, you'll continuously make sure that you have a seamless client experience and new products they will love to buy.

    o This leads to happy customers that stay and continue to buy beyond the initial offering.

    o As a result, you will create a higher and longer-term customer value and develop a brand that speaks for itself.

○ Hence, you will stay relevant and highly profitable in a changing marketplace.

○ You won't have to worry about "competition" anymore because you own a corner of the market.

- **Engaged Workforce:**

  ○ Your talent will feel valued, motivated, and connected to the company's success.

  ○ This will lead to a higher retention rate and productivity.

  ○ You can save at least 50 percent to 200 percent per talent.

- **Resilient Growth:**

  ○ Addressing conflicts and encouraging ideas from all levels creates a dynamic, future-proof organization.

  ○ You can leverage the knowledge that your operational people have to improve the quality of your product, your service, and your operations.

  ○ Hence, you won't feel stuck, not knowing how to solve your growth issue.

  ○ As a result, you can sleep peacefully and have a joyful dinner with your kids, knowing your team will always have your back and find solutions to the struggles the company is facing.

  ○ Imagine releasing the pressure of always having to be the one who comes up with solutions, which can be exhausting over time and will lead

LEÏLA LAHBABI

to starting to hate your company and not wanting to work on it anymore.

o I want to prevent you from getting to the stage where you say, "I don't care about this purpose anymore; I just want my peace back."

o You can have peace *and* a successful company.

COLLECTIVE INTELLIGENCE: TANGIBLE RESULTS

Whole Foods empowers its store teams to make localized decisions regarding product offerings and promotions. Employees participate in open forums to suggest improvements and vote on decisions that impact their work.

Whole Foods has:

- Consistent revenue growth, culminating in its $13.7 billion acquisition by Amazon

- High customer loyalty due to localized and personalized experiences

- Reduced employee turnover through an inclusive, empowering culture

- Customer-centric decision-making

Unilever integrates sustainability goals across teams by encouraging collaboration between supply chain, marketing, and R&D teams. Employees work together to reduce environmental impact while driving growth.

Unilever was able to:

- Achieve a 31 percent reduction in their carbon footprint across operations (2010–2020)

- Grow sustainability-focused brands like Dove and Ben & Jerry's that outperformed others, contributing to over 70 percent of growth

- Enhance their reputation among consumers and employees, improving brand equity and talent retention

Netflix has also embraced positive conflict resolution strategies and creativity. Netflix fosters a culture of candid feedback and radical transparency. Leaders encourage open discussions to address conflicts early, viewing disagreements as opportunities for innovation.

Netflix managed to:

- Expand from a DVD rental company to a global streaming powerhouse with over 230 million subscribers

- Continue to innovate with original content, leading to 226 Emmy nominations in 2023 alone

- Maintain a high-performance culture that attracts top talent and maintains creative excellence

Here are Five Steps to Build Collective Intelligence

1. Align Individual and Collective Objectives

Organizations flourish when personal ambitions harmonize with team goals. This alignment transforms your team into a unified force, fostering collaboration over competition and creating a shared sense of purpose.

Imagine the pride of leading a team where every individual knows their contribution drives not only their personal growth but also the collective mission. Witnessing your team work in harmony, driven by shared values, gives you the confidence that your organization is a place where people feel connected and inspired to give their best.

This alignment unlocks a culture of trust and innovation. Teams that collaborate rather than compete achieve break-throughs that propel the business forward faster and more sustainably. As a purpose-driven founder, you'll experience the relief of knowing your efforts to align personal and collective goals are building momentum toward meaningful progress.

Over time, this culture of alignment builds a workforce deeply committed to your vision. Talent stays loyal and energized by their meaningful contributions to a larger mission. You'll feel the profound satisfaction of scaling not just a company but a legacy: a thriving organization where collaboration drives sustainable growth, ensuring your purpose resonates far into the future.

2. Build a Mentorship Culture to Foster Psychological Safety

Mentorship transforms your organization into a community where every individual feels seen, valued, and supported. It creates an atmosphere of trust and psychological safety, allowing your team to ask for help, voice ideas, and collaborate without fear. Imagine the confidence and connection that grows when talent knows their contributions are celebrated, their voices matter, and they're empowered to thrive.

One of my clients reported a high performer refusing to collaborate, causing a ripple effect of declining team performance and morale. By introducing mentorship, the company built trust and fostered open communication, which reignited collaboration and improved overall productivity. The lesson? True performance lies not in individual achievements but in the ability to uplift the team and drive collective success.

Picture the pride and fulfillment of leading a business where mentorship creates a ripple effect of growth, trust, and engagement. This culture of mentorship strengthens collaboration, accelerates innovation, and increases team alignment. Talent feels empowered to grow, contribute, and lead, creating a workplace where trust fuels performance and passion ignites action.

Over time, this mentorship-driven culture ensures your organization's legacy of collaboration, trust, and purpose endures. As a founder, you'll experience the profound satisfaction of knowing your leadership has cultivated a company that uplifts everyone it touches.

3. Empower Innovation at Every Level

The secret to fostering innovation is engaging the people who are closest to the operational problems and encouraging them not only to execute but also to brainstorm better solutions. These are the talent who live and breathe the day-to-day tasks that, as you scale your company, you find yourself more removed from. The more you involve them, the more creative solutions you'll uncover because they're thinking about these problems every day.

Examples:

- **Toyota's Waigaya Sessions:** Anyone can call a meeting with executives to address challenges, which removes rank barriers.

- **Harley-Davidson's Freedom with Fences:** Talent is encouraged to challenge norms and explore new ideas.

- **REI's Store Visits:** Leaders gather feedback from front-line talent to shape strategy.

4. Balance Structure with Flexibility

Successful teams thrive on a foundation of structure that provides clear direction and purpose, yet they remain agile enough to embrace creativity and respond to challenges. As a purpose-driven founder, creating this balance allows you to lead with confidence, knowing your team has the discipline to execute effectively and the freedom to innovate without hesitation.

Imagine the deep satisfaction of seeing your vision realized through a team that operates like a finely tuned orchestra, each member aligned yet empowered to improvise when the moment calls for it. You're no longer burdened by micromanagement or chaos; instead, you witness a harmonious flow of productivity and ingenuity.

This balance builds resilience and adaptability within your organization. Clear structures ensure tasks are completed with precision, while flexibility fosters a culture of innovation and problem-solving. Teams feel secure knowing what's expected of them, but they also feel valued for their creative input and ability to navigate uncertainty.

Over time, this dynamic equilibrium positions your company as both dependable and forward-thinking. Clients, partners, and talent recognize your ability to deliver consistent results while staying ahead of industry trends. This trust transforms into lasting loyalty and collaboration, amplifying your mission and impact.

Ultimately, the legacy you build is one of sustainable growth and purpose. You'll feel the immense pride of knowing you've created an organization that not only achieves its goals but also inspires and uplifts everyone involved. It's a legacy of balance, creativity, and unwavering impact, a true reflection of your vision and values.

5. Address Conflicts with Kintsugi

This step is a game-changer. Since there's a bit to learn, keep reading to see how to apply it in your organization.

KINTSUGI AND CONFLICT RESOLUTION

Not discussing conflicts doesn't make them go away; it allows them to grow in the background, waiting for the moment they explode into a situation that may be beyond repair.

When I assess a new company, there's one question I always ask that tends to change the atmosphere in the room: "When was the last time you had an argument in your company?"

I always pause and deep dive when I have this answer: "We never argue."

To me, this is an immediate red flag that drives my attention to further exploration.

Although everything in this book emphasizes the importance of attracting people with shared values and purpose, I'm always dubitative about such a response. In almost every case, this claim hides a deeper issue: "We don't talk about how we feel openly to make sure we don't break what we've built."

Leaders who don't address this early on usually find themselves facing growing problems that they can no longer avoid. At that point, patience wears thin, and leaders are left frustrated and guilty for not speaking up sooner.

Be assured there is another way to handle this. I'm known for being direct, and while I've been learning to refine my communication over the years, what has always served me well is speaking my mind and heart. When received openly, it has helped me build stronger, more resilient relationships.

Avoiding conflicts only makes things worse. It turns minor issues into rumination, leading to bigger problems and altered realities. The longer you wait to address an issue, the harder it becomes to separate what truly happened from how you've interpreted it over time. By the time you do speak, the conversation may be completely out of sync because the other person may not even recall the original event.

But why do we avoid these conversations in the first place? Fear of breaking the relationship. We feel that addressing a conflict will damage the bond, but in reality, it can make the relationship stronger.

And here's the cost: US talent spends an average of *2.8 hours per week dealing with conflict,* which translates to a staggering *$359 billion in lost productivity annually* (CPP Inc.). Imagine how much unresolved conflicts are costing your business every single week.

The longer you let them fester, the more they drain your company's resources. There's an urgency to solving conflicts—not just to preserve relationships but to stop this constant leak in productivity. For every week a conflict remains unresolved, it continues to eat away at your performance and profitability.

There is a better way. I want to introduce a concept that can help shift your mindset on conflict: *Kintsugi*. This Japanese art form repairs broken pottery by mending the cracks with gold, creating a piece that is even more beautiful and valuable than before. In my own resilience journey, I've come to see that what doesn't break us can make us better—if we choose to mend those cracks with care and intention.

In every relationship, personal or professional, conflict is inevitable. However, like Kintsugi, addressing these breaks with gold—through mindful communication and empathy—can lead to stronger, more resilient teams. Unresolved conflicts will only grow; however, if we take the time to acknowledge and address them, we can transform these moments of tension into opportunities for collective growth and understanding.

PRACTICAL STEPS: BRINGING KINTSUGI TO THE WORKPLACE

Acknowledge the Breakage
Just like in Kintsugi, we must first recognize the conflict. This involves acknowledging the emotions and perspectives of everyone involved. Openly recognizing the issue is the first step toward repair.

Embrace the Cracks
In Kintsugi, the cracks aren't hidden but highlighted with gold. In your company, this means embracing differences and misunderstandings. By discussing the issues openly and with empathy, you can understand the root causes of the conflict and appreciate the diverse perspectives that your team members bring.

Repair with Gold
The gold in Kintsugi symbolizes healing. In the workplace, this translates to active listening, empathy, and constructive dialogue. Focus on finding solutions instead of assigning blame. When conflicts are addressed mindfully, they lead to stronger, more cohesive teams.

Create a Stronger Bond
Like the repaired pottery in Kintsugi, resolving conflicts through mindful communication builds stronger teams. Working through conflicts can deepen trust, respect, and connection among team members, ultimately enhancing collective performance.

By addressing conflicts head-on, you're not just solving problems; you're laying the foundation for a more resilient, high-performing organization. It's a proactive approach to ensuring that your team doesn't just survive but thrives. Ignoring conflicts is costly. It can lead to a 30 percent loss in productivity and a drastically decreased ability to retain talent. (Fifty percent of talent leave because of conflicts.) Solving conflicts is an investment in collective growth.

So, next time a conflict arises, remember Kintsugi. Embrace the cracks, repair with gold, and watch your team emerge stronger and more connected than ever. Solving conflicts will benefit both your short and long-term performance. We will get into more depth on short and long-term performance in general in the next chapter

The future belongs to companies that harness the full power of their people.

Scaling collective intelligence transforms organizations by unlocking potential far beyond individual achievements.

Aligning personal goals with team objectives, fostering mentorship, addressing conflicts openly, and empowering innovation ensure that everyone contributes meaningfully to the group's success.

The key to success lies in balancing structure with flexibility. Whether teams row in unison or improvise like a jazz band, collective intelligence enables organizations to thrive through collaboration, innovation, and resilience.

Scale Your Measure, Reflect, and Iterate

At this stage, you probably know me well enough to guess that I didn't write a whole book about how to scale your impact using a lean method and then ask you to use a rigid and overwhelming way to measure and iterate your performance.

Here again, I want to share a leaner way to measure, reflect, and iterate on your company's actions. However, before diving into the steps, I want to start by introducing the concepts with some use cases and the extraordinary results that come with them when you implement what we describe in this chapter.

Reflection and Growth Mindset Transformation at Microsoft

Under Satya Nadella, Microsoft shifted from a rigid performance-based culture to one rooted in a growth mindset. Regular feedback loops, reflective practices, and iterative improvements were embedded across teams, which:

- Reignited innovation, leading to a surge in cloud computing revenue and surpassing $60 billion annually

- Increased market capitalization from $300 billion to over $2.5 trillion within a decade

- Improved employee engagement and collaboration, fostering innovation across diverse business units

Kaizen for Continuous Improvement at Toyota

Toyota's Kaizen Approach focuses on incremental improvements across its operations. Front-line workers are empowered to suggest and implement changes, and metrics are continuously refined to reflect quality, efficiency, and customer satisfaction.

Here is what Toyota was able to achieve:

- **Reduction in Production Lead Times**: Toyota's human-centered manufacturing evolution and innovative technologies have led to a 50 percent reduction in equipment investment and production preparation lead time, along with a 20 percent increase in productivity (Toyota Europe).

- **Record Profit and Sales**: In the fiscal year ending March 2024, Toyota achieved a record net profit of 4.94 trillion yen (approximately $31.9 billion) and global sales exceeding 10.3 million units, driven by strong demand in markets such as North America, Europe, and Japan (Al Jazeera).

- **Milestone Hybrid Vehicle Sales**: By January 2020, Toyota surpassed 15 million cumulative hybrid electric vehicle sales worldwide, significantly reducing CO_2 emissions by more than 120 million tonnes compared to equivalent gasoline-powered vehicles (Toyota Newsroom).

Agile Iteration for Team Performance and Product Development at Spotify

Spotify uses the "Squad Model," which allows small, cross-functional teams to iterate quickly on product features. Reflection is embedded through retrospectives after every sprint, ensuring continuous learning and improvement.

Spotify was able to:

- Offer over 100 million tracks and more than 6 million podcasts, providing a diverse range of content to its users (Backlinko)

- Increase its total revenue in the third quarter of 2024 by 19 percent year-over-year, reaching €4 billion (Newsroom Spotify)

- Achieved a gross margin of 31.1 percent during the same period, reflecting improved profitability (Newsroom Spotify)

What can you learn from those examples and implement in your company context?

Moving From Peak Performance to Sustainable High Performance

In many organizations, performance is often seen as hitting peak after peak, delivering exceptional results repeatedly. However, this mindset can lead to a dangerous cycle, especially for top performers who are often overburdened, leading to burnout. One executive shared a common frustration: "Because you're a high-performing talent, you do a good job, and that means they put more on your plate. You have less and less time." This comes at the cost of your people's well-being, and their performance starts to decline.

Sustainable performance is about maintaining consistent, sustainable results over the long term without sacrificing talent well-being. It's also being able to have repeatable success. You set your company for success when you redefine what performance means by scaling measurement systems, building reflective practices, and embracing iterative improvement.

Redefining Performance Beyond the Peak

During a hike at Zion National Park in California, I noticed many hikers fixated on reaching the top. They rushed ahead, exhausted themselves, or stopped entirely, feeling overwhelmed by the distance. Instead of looking at the peak, I focused on maintaining a steady pace, enjoying the journey.

Two hikers followed my pace. By calmly focusing on each step (and enjoying the scenery), we all reached the summit, happier and more refreshed than those who had pushed too hard.

This experience reflects how focusing on steady growth, rather than fixating on the destination, can lead to greater success and more enjoyment along the way. It's the same with business. When you do your best, step by step, with ongoing reflection and celebration, you achieve more success effortlessly.

Performance isn't only about reaching a goal; it's about balancing short-term demands with long-term impact. Sustainable performance demands that you look beyond isolated achievements and create systems that support continuous growth.

I had the pleasure of interviewing an array of top leaders and CEOs for this book. As one interviewee put it, "Performance is not only the peak—the record; it's about having an impact, fostering relationships, and maintaining consistent results over time." Real success comes from achieving goals in ways that are sustainable, impactful, and aligned with core values.

SCALING MEASURES FOR LONG-TERM SUCCESS

"Do not judge yourself on your path of growth. Do not constantly evaluate yourself. A plant struggles to grow if you uproot it every morning to check its progress."

—Christiane Singer

Many companies fall into the trap of setting KPIs that focus too heavily on immediate gains, neglecting the foundational work that prepares them for future success. It's more effective to develop adaptable, scalable metrics that track not only short-term goals but also indicators of long-term health, such as talent engagement, cultural alignment, and innovation.

It's critical to measure the front-end metrics like sales or revenue and the entire value chain that drives sustainable growth to achieve this. This means leveraging the five levers of growth: number of contacts, conversion rates, number of transactions, value per transaction, and margin, not just from a commercial perspective but across all operational dimensions.

Add risk to that exposure if you have a business that involves taking financial risks like banking or insurance or if you have a business with a risk of non-payment or a high number of refund requests.

For example, you may have strong client numbers, high conversion rates, and good margins yet low transaction volume.

This could signal an operational bottleneck, such as limited delivery capacity, which might be solved by extending your team, adjusting your business model, or optimizing pricing strategies. By diagnosing problems across the value chain, brainstorming collective solutions, and testing them with input from operational experts and client insights, you create a system of rapid diagnosis and resolution.

KEY ACTIONS FOR SCALING MEASURES ACROSS THE VALUE CHAIN

1. **Diagnose Beyond the Surface**:

   o Diagnose deeply by leveraging your levers of growth to uncover bottlenecks or untapped potential across your operations.

   o By looking beyond front-end metrics to include efficiency, pricing, and delivery capacity, you ensure no opportunity is overlooked.

   o This approach provides the confidence to operate on solid, informed foundations, freeing you from the anxiety of unforeseen setbacks.

   o Addressing root issues enhances efficiency, aligns teams, and optimizes resources, creating a business that is both agile and resilient.

   o Over time, this holistic strategy fosters a self-sustaining system where challenges are preemptively resolved.

   o This allows your organization to scale effortlessly while staying true to its purpose.

2. **Collaborate Across Teams**:

   o Engage operational teams, stakeholders, and client-facing staff to uncover inefficiencies and co-create solutions, fostering open communication across the value chain.

   o As a purpose-driven founder, this collaboration deepens your connection to your mission and team, creating a shared sense of purpose and trust.

   o Co-creating solutions not only leads to more effective, actionable ideas but also boosts morale and team ownership, reducing turnover and building loyalty.

   o This culture of collaboration transforms your business into a resilient, adaptive ecosystem where challenges are proactively addressed.

   o You'll experience the fulfillment of leading a company where talent and stakeholders thrive together, united by their belief in your vision.

3. **Test and Iterate Rapidly:**

   o Implement small-scale tests to validate ideas before a broader rollout, using feedback from trials to refine and scale successful strategies.

   o This approach gives you confidence as a founder, ensuring decisions are grounded in real-world results rather than guesswork.

   o By scaling only proven solutions, you minimize risks, optimize resources, and drive progress efficiently.

o Over time, this iterative mindset fosters a culture of continuous improvement, embedding adaptability and learning into your organization's DNA.

o The pride of leading an innovative, results-driven business and witnessing your mission expand sustainably reaffirms your belief in your ability to scale with integrity and impact.

4. **Deal with Impatience:**

o Sometimes, you may have planted the right seeds in the right soil, but it just takes time for a plant to grow.

o Make sure not to remove a seed or cut a plant that was going to bring you fruits for years to come by being too short-term focused.

By incorporating the whole value chain into your measurement systems, you ensure your business remains adaptable and capable of scaling without sacrificing quality or operational efficiency.

This approach prepares your organization to make informed decisions at every level, driving both immediate wins and long-term sustainability.

LEARN FROM DOCTORS

Reflection is essential for long-term performance. Rather than relying solely on assessments or rigid personality tests, companies can foster reflective spaces that encourage personal and collective growth. By embedding regular reflection points, such as quarterly reviews or post-project debriefs, teams can learn from successes and challenges, fine-tuning their approaches along the way.

Reflection is similar to a doctor's check-up; it helps you diagnose issues early and course-correct them before they become problematic. By establishing regular check-ins, companies ensure they're always learning and improving rather than waiting for a crisis to prompt change.

KEY ACTIONS FOR EMBEDDING REFLECTION

- **Put Reflection on the Calendar (and Ensure Everyone Is on Board):**

    o By establishing regular reflection practices, such as quarterly or semi-annual reviews, you create a space where your team feels their efforts are valued, and their voices are heard.

    o This provides a profound sense of connection to your team's journey, reinforcing your role as a leader who prioritizes growth over unchecked hustle.

    o As these reviews uncover alignment with goals and highlight areas for improvement, your team gains a renewed sense of direction and purpose.

    o This clarity increases motivation, turning each milestone into a celebration of collective progress rather than a blurred step in an endless grind.

    o Over time, this rhythm of reflection strengthens your organization's resilience.

    o You'll witness a culture of accountability and learning emerge, where teams naturally course-correct and innovate.

o   As a founder, you'll feel the weight of reactive decision-making lift, replaced by the confidence of proactive, intentional growth.

- **Safety First:**

    o   Creating a safe environment for team discussions fosters trust and openness, allowing your talent to share successes, challenges, and lessons learned without fear.

    o   This builds an emotional bond with your team as you witness them grow not just professionally but personally within a supportive culture.

    o   When psychological safety becomes a cornerstone, your team is more likely to surface critical insights and propose bold ideas.

    o   This transparency strengthens problem-solving, boosts innovation, and aligns everyone more deeply with your mission.

    o   Over time, this safe, collaborative culture enhances team loyalty and engagement.

    o   Talent becomes deeply invested in the success of the company, translating to higher retention and a workforce that actively champions your vision.

    o   For you, it means scaling your impact with the assurance that your team is not only aligned but also thriving alongside you.

Time Management Isn't The Answer

Sustainable performance requires managing energy—not just hours. Time is limited, but energy levels fluctuate. By aligning work with talent's natural energy peaks, companies can increase productivity and prevent burnout.

I've experienced the pitfalls of pushing through long hours without energy management. My productivity often declined after extended focus. Traditional work structures emphasize hours, but energy management is about optimizing work for quality output.

Imagine, for example, a manager's day filled with back-to-back meetings. For a team leader, a 30-minute meeting might not be too draining. However, for an operational talent who is the most productive during focus time, that same 30-minute meeting may require additional recovery time to reconnect with their core work. Timing is also important. A meeting at 11:00 a.m. might cost more energy than a 2:00 p.m. meeting, especially for talent whose productive hours are in the morning.

The key to sustainable high performance lies in understanding these energy peaks and valleys and adjusting work patterns accordingly.

Recovery also plays a critical role here; embedding downtime, whether through flexible hours or shorter meetings, helps maintain momentum without risking burnout.

Going Beyond Rigid KPIs

Setting strict KPIs can actually stifle creativity. People aim low to ensure they hit their goals, or they feel disappointed if they don't meet their objectives. This approach narrows ambitions, restricts innovation, and makes success feel bi

Exclusively focusing on short-term KPIs can lead to quick wins but often comes at a cost to future growth. Short-term gains can create blind spots, making companies vulnerable to disruptions. Balancing short- and long-term KPIs ensures companies are succeeding today and preparing for future opportunities.

Disciplined execution is critical, but flexibility allows for greater potential. Talent should be trained to think beyond their KPIs, aiming for personal and collective growth rather than simply meeting numbers. Encouraging this growth mindset creates a culture of continuous improvement, where KPIs become tools, not constraints.

Empower your talent to see KPIs as stepping stones rather than limitations. Give them the freedom to stretch beyond their targets, trusting they'll aim higher when they're not confined to arbitrary limits.

Spotify's approach to growth and innovation reflects this mindset. If they had only focused on hitting specific revenue or subscriber targets each quarter, they might have optimized for short-term ad revenue or subscription sales. Instead, they prioritized *user experience, personalization, and innovation,* which led to groundbreaking features like Discover Weekly and Wrapped. Their willingness to experiment beyond rigid financial KPIs has helped them redefine the music industry and sustain long-term customer engagement.

By focusing on continuous improvement rather than rigid performance metrics, Spotify has created a culture where innovation thrives. Their teams are encouraged to think beyond fixed targets and instead push the boundaries of what's possible, leading to long-term growth and industry leadership.

Fostering Iteration for Adaptability

Iteration is about embracing change and learning through continuous adjustments. Companies can encourage a culture of iteration—where goals, metrics, and strategies are continuously refined to respond to market shifts and internal learnings.

Key Actions for Fostering Iteration:

- **Adopt Flexible Goals**:

  - Adopting flexible goals transforms them into dynamic milestones that evolve with changing circumstances, customer feedback, and team insights.

  - This approach reduces the stress of rigid plans, fosters trust, and empowers your team to align with shifting priorities, driving innovation and resilience.

  - By embracing adaptability, your business becomes nimble and thrives in an ever-changing market, creating a sustainable growth trajectory.

  - The result is the emotional fulfillment of watching your mission expand without losing its essence, guided by a proactive team fully invested in driving your vision forward.

- **Incorporate Feedback Loops**:

  - Integrating structured feedback loops into your operations ensures that decisions, product iterations, and process improvements are guided by real-world insights from customers, team members, and market trends.

o This approach eliminates the uncertainty of operating in isolation, deepens your connection to your mission, and accelerates improvements across your business.

o By fostering a culture of listening and responding, you enhance customer loyalty, team engagement, and operational efficiency.

o Over time, these feedback loops create a self-sustaining cycle of growth and innovation.

o This provides the emotional satisfaction of knowing your business evolves in harmony with its stakeholders and amplifies its impact.

WHAT IT TAKES TO CREATE A CULTURE OF RECOGNITION

Recognition is an essential part of scaling performance. It isn't just about boosting morale; recognition reinforces positive behavior and creates psychological safety. When talent feels seen and valued, they're more engaged and willing to contribute at a high level. Publicly recognizing achievements also strengthens team bonds and helps embed a positive, sustainable culture.

Key Actions

- **Make Recognition Public and Frequent**:
  o Public and frequent recognition turns accomplishments into shared moments of pride and inspiration, fostering collaboration and strengthening team bonds.

o By celebrating successes, creating awards, and encouraging peer-to-peer recognition, you boost morale and motivate employees to sustain high performance.

o For a purpose-driven founder, witnessing these celebrations brings deep fulfillment as you build a thriving, supportive community where individual growth aligns with the company's mission.

o Over time, this culture of recognition attracts top talent, enhances retention, and transforms your organization into a proud, high-performing workforce, amplifying your vision and reinforcing your impact.

- **Align Recognition with Company Values:**

  o Recognizing achievements that align with your company's mission integrates values into everyday actions, celebrating not just results but the purpose-driven approach behind them.

  o This fosters a culture where ethical behavior and mission-driven excellence are rewarded, strengthening employees' connection to your vision.

  o As a founder, seeing your values embodied in your team's work brings deep satisfaction and reinforces the principles that inspired your organization.

  o Over time, this alignment builds a reputation for authenticity and integrity, attracting clients, partners, and talent who resonate with your purpose and creating lasting pride and fulfillment as you lead a truly mission-driven company.

How To Sustain High Performance Without Burning People Out

Scaling performance sustainably requires shifting from peak-focused output to a balanced approach. By scaling measures, fostering reflection, and encouraging iteration, organizations can create a culture that values steady growth, adaptability, and resilience. This ensures that teams are not only achieving immediate goals but are also laying the groundwork for future success.

In adopting these principles, organizations empower their talent to do their best work—measured by results, guided by reflection, and continuously iterated to meet evolving challenges.

Scale Your Ability to Exit

If you cannot step away from your business, you haven't built a business; you've built a job. When you focus on daily operations without preparing the business to thrive independently, you risk creating a fragile organization that relies on your presence.

An important part of scaling your ability to exist is preparing for your succession. If you don't have a structured approach to leadership succession, your company becomes heavily dependent on you, making it unsellable or unattractive to investors. It becomes nearly impossible to detach because your business is adapted around you instead of operating as an independent, resilient entity. Ultimately, this makes it harder to convince investors that you have a capable team in place to support growth and scalability.

Scaling your ability to exit starts now and prepares your business for:

1. **Raising Money**
   Investors want to invest in a business—not a job. When you show that your business can operate without your constant involvement, supported by a strong team and a clear succession plan, you increase investors' confidence in your business by increasing your company's financial evaluation and your chances to raise more money while keeping the highest percentage of ownership in your business.

2. **CEO Succession**
   As your company grows, a pivotal moment arrives when considering appointing a new CEO to sustain and expand the company's impact, which is an important move to enhance your business and your life. This ensures continuity and strengthens your company's foundation beyond your direct influence.

3. **Selling or Running Seamlessly Without You**
   Creating a self-sustaining business with independent leadership and solid processes makes your company far more attractive for acquisitions and outside investment. Even if you don't want to sell your business, it enables you to keep it while keeping the advantages and minimizing the burden.

In this chapter, you will see how you can scale your ability to detach yourself from your business through establishing CEO successions, addressing family-run business succession, and investing in your people to support scalability.

LEADERSHIP SUCCESSION WITH CONTINUITY OF DNA

In the early stages, the founder often plays the dual role of both founder and CEO. However, as the company grows, a pivotal moment arrives when you must decide whether to bring in a new leader to maintain and expand the company's impact.

Here is how you can do it in a way that includes actions we discussed during the first four steps of the Impact at Scale Approach:

1. **Select a Mission-Aligned Successor**

   o   Identify a successor who understands your mission and can translate it into a scalable set of actions.

   o   This choice is about more than finding a competent executive; it's about choosing someone who embodies your approach and can make decisions as you would, even in your absence.

   o   Your successor must teach the company to act with your principles as a guide, ensuring your influence endures.

   o   Step 1, Scaling your Mission, makes this action easier.

2. **Build a Talent Pool Around You and Your Successor**

   o   Create a group of leaders who can operate as extensions of your mindset.

   o   These leaders should be able to make decisions, challenge, and be challenged, ensuring their actions align with your company's values and purpose.

176

- o This framework fosters leadership continuity without direct dependence on you.

- o Step 2, Scaling Your Talent Attraction and Retention, and Step 4, Scaling Your Talent Performance, make this action easier.

3. **Train for Cascading Leadership**

   - o Develop leadership at every level of the organization.

   - o This model ensures that as the business evolves, new leaders can introduce fresh ideas while still aligning with your vision.

   - o Leadership flows down through multiple levels, ensuring all leaders uphold your company's purpose, values, and culture, enabling adaptability and resilience without losing sight of its core identity.

   - o This has been addressed in Step 3, Scaling the CEO, and Step 4, Scaling the Team Performance.

ADDRESS FAMILY-RUN BUSINESS SUCCESSION

Family-run businesses, often built on deep personal connections, face unique hurdles when it comes to leadership transitions and scaling.

The statistics are telling: Only 30 percent of family businesses survive the transition from first to second-generation ownership, and just 12 percent make it to the third generation.

Additionally, 47 percent of family business owners expecting to retire within five years do not have a successor lined up.

This is a critical issue that highlights the importance of succession planning and family dynamics in business.

A family business is often the result of the founder's heart, purpose, vision, and values, which they pass on to their family. However, things can get complicated when a new generation steps in to lead. Much like when a new executive joins a company and attempts to replicate past success without understanding the new environment, a generational shift in leadership can lead to internal conflict and operational dysfunction.

Here is what scale your ability to exit means in a family-run business:

1. **Prepare for Family Dynamics in Leadership**

    o Actively engage in succession planning, aligning family and business goals and addressing internal conflicts to avoid operational dysfunction.

2. **Create Harmony or Set Boundaries**

    o If family members are involved, encourage collaborative relationships and recognize complementary skills.

    o Alternatively, establish clear boundaries and responsibilities to avoid potential conflicts, or if harmony can't be achieved, consider exiting the business to preserve its legacy.

3. **Prepare the Next Generation**

    o If you wish to pass the business to your children, integrate them into operations early so they absorb the company's challenges and values firsthand.

o Successors should lead in a way that reflects their strengths while honoring their legacy and preserving the business's core values while adapting to future demands.

o Also, you cannot lie to your kids about your work-life balance and running a business being one of the most fun activities. Your actions and feelings tell more than your words—especially if they have been witnessing that since a young age:

  ▪ Were you at their sports games and school events?

  ▪ Were you there to pick them up from school and go have an ice cream together?

  ▪ How did you spend the weekends?

  ▪ Did you have fun with your kids, or were you always worried about your business?

Family business founders come to me confused about why their kids don't want to take their business successions.

My answer to them is, "They are not lazy; they are disappointed."

If you follow the Impact at Scale Approach I describe throughout this book, you'll drastically reduce the probability that it will happen.

4. **Consider External Investor Dynamics**

o When introducing external investors, wisely choose those who respect your family's values and mission.

○ Investors can be either a support or a source of tension; ensure alignment to prevent conflicts that could affect decision-making and business direction.

○ Be aware that introducing external investors makes them a part of your business and your decision-making. Make peace with that, or don't do it. This is an option if you want to go there, but not the only one to keep your business growing without you, so don't force yourself into it if you don't feel it.

There are many examples of successful family-run businesses and some less successful transitions. LVMH, led by Bernard Arnault, is a great case study of how family members can work together to scale a global empire. Arnault has involved his children in the business while preparing them to lead in the future.

On the other hand, Bill Gates has chosen to allow his children to pursue their own paths, showing a different approach to family legacy and business succession.

There is not one approach. In the Billion-Dollar Purpose Approach, I encourage you to listen to your heart and pursue the path that will take you there, being aware of the different possibilities that are offered to you and not waiting to start thinking about and preparing your ability to exit.

Similarly, as talent prepares for retirement every day of their working life, you want to prepare for your exit every day of your business life.

INVEST IN YOUR PEOPLE TO SUPPORT SCALABILITY

In a conversation with an expert on scaling companies and investor exits, one fact stood out: 20 to 25 percent of a company's financial evaluation during due diligence depends on its people. This isn't just about the numbers on paper; it's about leadership, team dynamics, and the ability to foster long-term growth. Eighty percent of startups fail, not because of the market or product but because of people—the lack of leadership, poor decision-making, and fragile group cohesion. If leadership and teams are not built on solid foundations, no product or financial strategy will compensate.

The ability to attract and retain high-performing talent directly impacts a company's longevity and scalability. People management is not a nice-to-have; it's a fundamental driver of performance. As part of an investor's evaluation, assessing leadership isn't just about determining if the management team is competent; it's about figuring out whether they are the reason the company thrives or if they're holding it back.

Investors will ask, "Is this leadership team an asset, or will the company benefit more from new leadership?" Don't wait until you're ready to sell your company to fix the people aspect. Start investing in your talent now so that if the time comes to sell or bring in investors, your company is far more attractive.

Here is what you can start doing now:

1. **Strengthen People's Due Diligence**

   o Given that a company's valuation depends heavily on its people, it is crucial to invest in leadership and team development early.

- o A business reliant on your direct oversight weakens its long-term scalability.

- o Strengthen your team to operate independently, attracting investors who see a robust and resilient organization.

2. **Lay the Foundation for Independence**

- o Like raising a child, guide, teach, and provide structure to enable your team to eventually operate without your constant involvement.

- o Investing in your people builds a self-sustaining business, allowing you to step back without disrupting performance.

- o You should enjoy the journey of growing your business, viewing this investment as a way to gain both personal freedom and a stronger company.

3. **Embed People-Centric Values**

- o Establish a culture that prioritizes talent attraction, training, and retention.

- o This approach drives performance and enhances morale and loyalty, making your business appealing to investors and acquirers alike.

Imagine the benefits for your business:

- • **Investor Appeal and Higher Valuation**

  - o Investors are drawn to businesses that are not dependent on their founders, valuing independence, scalability, and an established leadership team.

- o The result is a higher valuation and a smoother process for both investments and acquisitions.

- **Your Flexibility**

  - o When your business can operate independently, you gain the freedom to scale back your involvement or shift your focus, trusting the company will continue to thrive.

- **Long-Term Sustainability**

  - o With a solid foundation and embedded leadership, your business gains resilience.

  - o This ensures it can withstand changes in leadership and adapt to new market challenges without losing its core identity.

- **Enhanced Team Morale and Productivity**

  - o A robust leadership structure boosts morale.

  - o When talent feels empowered and engaged, they contribute to an adaptable, growth-oriented culture.

- **Legacy Beyond You**

  - o By building a business that operates independently of you, the organization becomes a lasting legacy.

  - o That can continue to impact long after your departure, fulfilling its mission sustainably.

By adopting these strategies, you can create a business that thrives autonomously, scaling impact and legacy without compromising values, culture, or mission.

The impact of your work in this world will continue to scale after you leave the business and the world.

The time to start is now. Build, attract, retain, and train, but also have a lot of fun while doing it.

As we wrap up this book, I want to equip you with practical tools to help you implement the strategies we've explored. To support you on this journey, I've created cheat sheets that summarize the step-by-step action plan for each key concept. You can access them here: leilalahbabi.com/impactatscalecheatsheets.

These cheat sheets are designed for clarity and efficiency, ensuring you can take meaningful action without feeling overwhelmed.

Cheers to your success and fulfillment!

WRAPPING IT ALL UP: BOTH HANDS CLAP-ING

As we come to the end of this book, it's important to take a moment to reflect on the essence of what we've explored together. The journey of scaling *Billion-Dollar Purpose* is not simply about ticking boxes or achieving KPIs; it's about cultivating something deeper, something that will last.

At the beginning of the book, I promised to show you how we can scale *Billion-Dollar Purpose* without burning out by attracting, training, and retaining high-performing teams in a way that compounds results over time. Now that you've explored these strategies, I'm excited for you to take them forward in your journey.

Why This Matters

- Only 1 percent of companies successfully scale.

- Eighty percent of startups fail not due to the market or product but because of people—lack of leadership, poor decision-making, and weak group cohesion.

- Purpose-driven companies are ten times more financially successful than S&P 500 companies.

- Twenty to twenty-five percent of a company's valuation during due diligence depends on its people.

Remember the Moroccan proverb I shared at the beginning of this book?

"One hand doesn't clap."

This is why CLAP is a great way to summarize the impact of the approach highlighted in this book.

THE CLAP FRAMEWORK

C – Collective Intelligence: Companies with strong collective performance systems experience a *20 percent increase in profitability* (Deloitte, *Global Human Capital Trends*).

L – Leadership: Companies with strong leadership development see a *30 percent improvement in performance* (McKinsey, *Leadership Effectiveness Study*).

A – Autonomy: Autonomous teams experience a *40 percent productivity increase* compared to centrally controlled ones (MIT Sloan Review).

P – People: Talent retention and engagement enable a *21 percent increase in productivity.*

THE COMPOUNDING EFFECT: A 2.6 TIMES PERFORMANCE MULTIPLIER

By integrating these principles, your company can multiply its performance by 2.6 times year after year. The result isn't just additive; it's compounding and exponential!

Final Performance Impact Equation:

$C * L * A * P = 1.20 * 1.25 * 1.40 * 1.21 = 2.537$

This translates to achieving *over 153 percent better company performance*, the number I promised to explain at the end of the chapter.

S – Sustainability: Long-term business resilience—financially, environmentally, and culturally—ensures companies that embed sustainability into their leadership strategy consistently outperform those focused only on short-term gains.

This results in a **100 times performance multiplier in five years.**

While this formula is a simplified representation combining different performance metrics (profitability, financial gains, and productivity), it directionally illustrates the power of compounding leadership improvements. By embedding these principles into your business, you're not just adding value; you're multiplying it.

YOUR NEXT STEPS

If you've made it to the end of this book and haven't yet downloaded the Billion-Dollar Cheatsheets, you can finish your reading with them here: leilalahbabi.com/billiondollarpurposecheatsheets.

If you want additional support beyond this book, feel free to contact me here: contact@leilalahbabi.com or connect with me on LinkedIn for more insights: linkedin.com/in/leilalahbabiimpactstrategy.

Final Thoughts

As you move forward, I encourage you to keep one key thought in mind: *Enjoy the journey.* Whether it's the small victories, the challenging moments, or the milestones that define your company's growth, each step brings you closer to building something remarkable, lasting, and truly impactful.

Here's to the future you're building—one intentional decision, one empowered team, and one conscious step at a time. The real work begins now, and I can't wait to see the impact you create.

ABOUT THE AUTHOR

Leïla Lahbabi is a former strategy consultant turned conscious leadership advisor, entrepreneur, and speaker. After years of supporting CEOs and investors at Oliver Wyman in building growth strategies, she realized that the biggest lever for sustainable success or accelerator of failure was people.

Leïla is the founder of MINDIMPACT and MINDFU-LACADEMY, platforms that help purpose-driven leaders scale themselves and their businesses through high-performing talent, leadership autonomy, and values-aligned cultures. Her clients include impact startups, growing scale-ups, and conscious investors.

As an engineer, mathematician, psychologist, trained mindfulness practitioner and advocate of conscious capitalism, Leïla brings together strategic clarity and human insight to help organizations scale profitably and purposefully. Her approach is deeply rooted in her own transformation, navigating burnout, personal loss, and the search for a more meaningful form of success.

With *Billion Dollar Purpose*, she offers a new playbook for founders, investors, and changemakers who want to scale high impact and low burn-out profitable companies where both people and the planet thrive.

ACKNOWLEDGMENTS

Writing this book has been a transformative journey, and there are many people without whom this project would not have come to life.

First, I want to thank all the leaders, CEOs, managers, and entrepreneurs who generously shared their experiences with me. Your candid stories, wisdom, and insights enriched every page of this book. You didn't just provide answers; you brought real-world lessons that I hope will inspire and guide others the way they have guided me.

To my clients, you have been my greatest teachers. Working with you, seeing your evolution, and witnessing your businesses thrive has given me profound insight into what it takes to grow high-performing teams. I am endlessly grateful for your trust and the privilege of walking with you on your journey.

A heartfelt thank you goes to my family and loved ones. You have been my solid ground through every step, patiently enduring the time when my mind was lost in writing. Your love, encouragement, and unwavering belief in me gave me the strength to persevere, even when it seemed difficult to balance everything.

A special mention goes to the incredible professionals—the editors, proofreaders, and all those who worked behind the scenes. Your dedication and attention to detail made this book sharper, clearer, and more impactful. Thank you for helping me articulate my vision in the best possible way.

To every reader who picks up this book, whether you're here for inspiration, guidance, or curiosity, I wrote this for you. My hope is that it guides you toward creating workplaces that not only succeed but also nurture the people within them. Your commitment to learning and growth is what drives change in organizations, and I am honored to be part of your journey.

Finally, to the people and experiences that taught me the value of resilience, mindfulness, and human connection, you are the unseen yet deeply felt contributors to this work. Thank you for the lessons that shaped my approach to leadership and life.

May we continue to learn, grow, and build better businesses together.